B

If your days feel more life-draining than life-giving, let Susie Larson show you how to reclaim the joyful, fruitful life God wants for you.

—**Mark Batterson,** bestselling author
and lead pastor of National Community Church

Susie really opened my eyes to look for God's best when deciding where I spend my time. He doesn't give up on us because we made mistakes. He has a design and purpose to fulfill, and the enemy would love nothing more than to take us out with exhaustion and wasted time.

—**Caroline Barnett,** co-pastor of The Dream Center
and author of *Willing to Walk on Water*

Saying yes to God is the most important decision you can make, but it shouldn't stop there. After beginning a relationship with Christ, we must constantly say yes to His influence, wisdom, and power in our lives. *Your Sacred Yes* will empower and equip you to say yes to a life of freedom, fulfillment, and significance. Say yes!

—**Craig Groeschel,** senior pastor of LifeChurch.tv
and author of *From This Day Forward*

Challenging us to carefully consider our sacred responsibilities, Susie Larson uses her trademark transparent stories to compel us to rest more and to make the difficult decisions that will prioritize our relationship with God. If you find yourself in the rat race of life, *Your Sacred Yes* will give you the courage to slow down and say yes to the right things.

—**Pastor Nate and Jodi Ruch,** Emmanuel Christian Center

This is such a timely book for all of us. I am grateful that Susie said yes to writing these sacred truths. This book will strengthen and empower all of us to follow the voice of God with more boldness and clarity.

—**Brady Boyd,** pa
and au

D0187497

Your Sacred

Yes

Books by Susie Larson

Your Sacred Yes

Trading Life-Draining Obligation for
FREEDOM, PASSION & JOY

SUSIE LARSON

BETHANY HOUSE PUBLISHERS

a division of Baker Publishing Group
Minneapolis, Minnesota

© 2015 by Susie Larson

Published by Bethany House Publishers
11400 Hampshire Avenue South
Bloomington, Minnesota 55438
www.bethanyhouse.com

Bethany House Publishers is a division of
Baker Publishing Group, Grand Rapids, Michigan

Printed in the United States of America

Library of Congress Cataloging-in-Publication Data
Larson, Susie
    Your sacred yes : trading life-draining obligation for freedom, passion, and joy / Susie Larson.
       pages cm
    Includes bibliographical references.
    Summary: "Radio host Susie Larson invites women to focus their time and passion on sacred and significant areas of life instead of allowing overcommitment and busyness to determine their self-worth"—Provided by publisher.
    ISBN 978-0-7642-1331-1 (pbk. : alk. paper) 1. Christian women—Religious life. 2. Self-realization—Religious aspects—Christianity. 3. Christian life. I. Title.
    BV4527.L3773 2015
    248.8′43—dc23   2014047139

Cover design by LOOK Design Studio

Author is represented by The Steve Laube Agency

15 16 17 18 19 20 21   7 6 5 4 3 2 1

To my husband, Kevin—
Your constant and continual love and strength
have provided me grace and space to give my full yes to God.
Thank you, honey. Next to Jesus, you're my very best thing.
I'll love you forever.

To our families, the Ericksons and the Larsons—
We love you dearly.

To my Savior, Jesus—
Where would I be without Your love?
After walking with You all these years,
I finally understand that
You're far kinder than I can fathom
and more powerful than I can imagine.
I'll love and follow You forever.

Contents

9

Foreword

Susie Larson had me from the first paragraph of this book! By the end of the first page, she had already succeeded in making me want to become a different person who drinks from a deeper and quieter well. As one who reads dozens of books a year, I can't tell you how unusual this is for me, which is why I begged Susie early on to rework this book to include addressing men. In its early incarnation, *Your Sacred Yes* addressed wives, mothers, sisters, and daughters; I pleaded with Susie that husbands, fathers, brothers, and sons needed to hear this searing truth as much as any woman alive. If you're a man who is reading this, you're very welcome!

As an ardent fan of the Christian classics, I've been challenged by my brothers and sisters in the Eastern Orthodox tradition who define "lust" radically differently than do modern evangelicals. If you say the word *lust* in a North American church today, 99.9 percent of the congregation will assume you're talking about sexual desire of some sort. In the Eastern classics, sex isn't the most destructive or pervasive lust—the fear of man and the desire for praise and approval is.

I've been convicted by this truth, but Susie helped me see this in a contemporary context that empowered me in a way I hadn't quite experienced before. She took me by the hand, peeled back the layers of my pride and approval lust, and gently told me, "You don't have to stay there. There's another place—a better place—out of which you can live more freely, more productively, more joyfully." Perhaps because of my own book titles, Susie's line "I refuse the rat race because God has called me to the sacred race" hit me as hard (in a good way) as anything I've ever read.

I usually race through the books I'm asked to endorse—the deadline in the front of my mind. But in this case, I felt God telling me to hold this book to a chapter a day. "This book is for you," He seemed to say (putting it in my own words). "Let it become a part of you. Let it nurture your spirit. You need to hear this."

Matthew 6:33 ("Seek first the kingdom of God" NKJV) and John 4:34 ("My food is to do the will of him who sent me and to finish his work") comprise every true Christian's calling. We get one life on this earth. Susie invites us to imbue each day with sacred meaning, sacred purpose, God-ordered delight, and the freedom of worshiping the only One whose opinion ultimately matters. That's a glorious platform from which to live. Her writing is steeped in scriptural understanding and discernment. Though she quotes plenty of Scriptures, even when she doesn't, you recognize the biblical priorities and instruction that have shaped her mind and gracefully challenge us.

Thank you, Susie, for this gift to the church and for calling each citizen of heaven to focused service, grace-based obedience, and the freedom of walking Christ's path.

Gary Thomas
Bestselling author of *Sacred Marriage*
and international speaker

Introduction

Are We Missing It?

I have a question for you: *Are we missing it?* Have we as God's people—who endure this crazy-paced culture—given away a mindset that *looks for and enjoys* the presence of God? Have we allowed the precious gift of expectancy to slip through our fingers? How often do we cup our hand to our ear and listen for heaven's song over our lives? Are we so bogged down with life-draining commitments that we've forgotten how good a belly laugh feels or how rich a time of quiet prayer can be? Do we relegate praise and worship to an hour on Sunday and thereby miss out on singing at the top of our lungs every other day of the week? Has it occurred to us that God longs for us to take a more life-giving path than the one we're on?

Sometimes we overcommit for all the wrong reasons (pride, insecurity, fear, hastiness). Other times we have the best of intentions for giving away our time (a good cause, a great need, there's nobody else). Either way, we need to ask ourselves some probing questions:

- Do the vast majority of our yeses increase our faith and fill us with a greater expectancy of how God is moving in our midst? Or do they drain us to the point that we find ourselves weary, simply rushing from one thing to the next?

- Are we captive to our commitments, or free to respond to God's invitation to do life with Him?
- Is our current path a catalyst to increasing joy and faith, or does all of our rushing make us more prone to worry and fear?
- When we assess honestly the time we give away to our various commitments, do we find behind it all a divinely inspired soul growing in grace and strength? Or are we a spent and weary soul, losing steam by the day?

Nothing drains us more than signing up for things God never asked us to do. Yet all too often that's exactly where we lose our way. When we live shackled to others' opinions, expectations, and requirements, we give away our yes because of a lie. We commit to things in order to save face, and as a result, we miss out on God's invitation to fully entrust ourselves to Him.

Days will fly by and sacred moments will continue to elude us until we decide to hit the brakes and take inventory of what's driving us.

Consider this book an invitation to break free from the bondage of others' opinions, overcommitment, and the un-appointed obligations that drain us dry and steal our joy. It's time to reclaim our days so that our moments matter in the greater scheme of things. Both our no's and our yeses matter to God because He loves us best and He's the one who can make the most of our days and our moments.

I don't want to miss one thing the Lord has for me. How about you? First Corinthians 4:20 says this: "For the kingdom of God is not a matter of talk but of power."

The kingdom of God isn't just a theory we discuss, nor is it just a list of do's and don'ts that we must carefully obey. Instead, it's a living, breathing relationship with Jesus, the Most High God who intends to transform us from the inside out, mark our lives with power, show us where to go, and use us in ways completely disproportionate to who we are.

Sadly, once we've secured our eternity, far too many of us live like the rest of the world. We rush from one thing to the next. We worry about the same things the lost world does. We enslave ourselves to the same things many others are addicted to. We commit ourselves to lots of things—many of them good things, but things God never asked us to commit to.

When we forget—or become too busy—to tap in to the provision and power God has made available to us, we find ourselves weary, rushed, earthbound people who merely react to our circumstances. From the outside looking in, we look like everybody else—tired, overworked, and underjoyed.

But Jesus invites us to live as joyful, secure, expectant people who respond to the nudges of the Holy Spirit within us, who live awakened to the adventure of faith God invites us to, and who believe that as kingdom people, everywhere we place our feet, the spiritual atmosphere changes because Christ-in-us has led us there.

Jesus invites us to walk intimately with Him, to abide with Him and in Him in such a way that our life abounds in life-giving fruit—solid evidence that we're connected to a supernatural Source. He invites us to experience His kingdom power mightily at work in us, through us, and all around us. That's the invitation.

Life is a gift. Time is a treasured commodity. When we open our hands and give what we have to Jesus—be it our moments, our gifts, our time, or simply room and space for Him to show up—we find life to be a sacred journey.

When we do life with a consistent awareness of God's presence in our midst, we find joy. And that's the place where healing, fulfillment, and abundance happen. Jesus invites us to live purposeful and passionate, focused and free. It's time to grab hold of our moments and cherish our days the way Jesus cherishes us. I don't want to miss a thing He has for us, do you? I didn't think so. I so look forward to making this journey with you.

With joyful expectancy,
Susie Larson

How to Use This Book

Please use this book in a way that most suits you. If you grow best in the context of a Bible study group, approach this as a six-week study, and complete two chapters each week. Reflection Questions and Discussion Starters are provided after each chapter, and you will find in-depth Bible study questions in a **Workbook** that can be downloaded at www.susielarson.com.

Also available separately is a **DVD Study Companion** that includes six twenty-five-minute segments that cover and expand on the material in this book, two chapters at a time. Together, the book, workbook, and DVD allow groups to host a six-week study at home or church.

Please note: Some of the Reflection Questions and Discussion Starters probe deeply and may feel too personal to address with others unless you're with your closest confidants. You decide what to share. You may prefer to read the book during your alone times with God and talk your way through it with a few close friends.

Either way, I encourage you not to take this journey alone. Invite others to stand with you, pray with you, and spur you on as you reclaim for God the sacred areas of your life.

THE SLOPPY

Yes

❖ 1 ❖

Caution: Danger Ahead

Say Yes to God's Wisdom

Guard your heart above all else, for it determines
the course of your life.

Proverbs 4:23 NLT

Sin is not where the enemy most often gets his foot-
hold on the godly. Rather . . . the enemy more often
latches on to weakness—or maybe I should say a
hidden spot of vulnerability. Of course, Satan knows
that weakness can turn to sin in a heartbeat when
exposed to just the right amount of pressure.[1]

Beth Moore

Years ago I responded to a breakfast invitation from a woman I
had recently met. She'd read my first book, had watched me from
a distance, and wanted to talk with me. I looked forward to getting to know a new friend. I had no idea I was about to receive

a wake-up call that almost knocked me silly. Our eggs and hash-browns sat untouched on our plates. She leaned across the table with purposefulness and proceeded to tell me her story—how she and her husband once served in visible leadership roles (like my husband and me), and how people honored and respected them for all of their contributions (again, like us), and how, for a season, all of their activity bore huge amounts of fruit (like us, it seemed).

Then, one day, it happened. In a moment of sheer exhaustion and unrealized vulnerability, her husband lost his footing, tripped up morally, and everything came crashing down around them. At the time she and I met, they were still sorting through the wreckage, trying to put their life back together. She leaned closer and said: "Susie, I'm quite sure that neither Kevin nor you have any thoughts or secret desires to step off of God's best path for you. But I see the weariness in your eyes, and I know we have a fierce opponent who is our enemy. He'll wait for just the right time to trip you or Kevin up. He intends to take you out. God has put you on my heart time and time again, and I'm telling you, warning you, please step back, get some rest, reset, and put some firmer boundaries around your marriage, your life, and your time."

That breakfast date put a healthy fear of God in me. I believe it's entirely possible that she saved us from some kind of devastation, and I thank God for her courage. Kevin and I were racing toward burnout at the time, and that encounter was one of the catalysts God used to slow us down and put us back on track. Since then, we've maintained certain marriage and time boundaries.

Thankfully, God loves us all enough to alert us to the enemy traps and dangers down the road. May we be wise enough to listen to the messages He sends our way and make the necessary course adjustments.

The prudent see danger and take refuge, but the simple keep going and pay the penalty.

Proverbs 27:12

When we—without thinking too much about it—give away our time to things un-appointed by God, we will *not* have the grace to sustain them. Consequently, we put ourselves at risk of the enemy's schemes. We may forge ahead with energy and enthusiasm, but, under our own strength, we're not strong enough to keep our own footing. Especially when we live out from under God's best will for us.

We need Jesus every hour—and for good reason. We need Him because without Him, we fall into the traps the enemy sets for us. And by extension, we miss out on the life of precious intimacy God invites us to enjoy *with Him*. We follow the Shepherd because He guards and guides us with the utmost care. He teaches us as we follow Him. And He draws us so close that our hearts actually begin to beat in rhythm with His. A with-Him kind of life is what He intended for us from the beginning of time.

> My eyes are always on the Lord, for he rescues me from the traps of my enemies.
>
> Psalm 25:15 NLT

Where Are You Vulnerable?

A great chasm exists between an abundantly full, fruitful life and a strained, drained, busy life. We'll explore the invitation to faith-filled abundance in a later chapter. But for now, let's look at the impact of the kind of busyness that leaves us vulnerable and exposed to the enemy's schemes. The Chinese word for *busyness* combines two symbols made up of these two words: *heart killer*. So true. I know from personal experience how dangerous and draining overcommitment can be. Like a slow death, my overcommitment all those years ago killed my passions, my perspective, and my sense of calling, leaving me weak, tired, and disillusioned. Maybe you can relate.

Several months ago I decided to cover the topic of spiritual vulnerability on my radio show. The phones lit up, and listeners called in to share about their near misses, their failures, and the steps they now take to guard their hearts. I'll never forget one particular call that came in that day. The woman, who wished to be anonymous, shared how both she and her husband had been busy running parallel paths, doing life simultaneously but separately. Then she met a man. She choked on her words as she attempted to share the rest of her story. "I mistakenly believed that the burden of my obedience to God—given the current state of my marriage—would be heavier than the consequence of my sin," she said. "But I couldn't have been more wrong. It would have been far easier to resist temptation than to face what I'm dealing with now."

I've heard this same story countless times from solid, engaged Christians who felt suddenly blindsided by temptation and vulnerability—and seemingly out of nowhere. Over and over again, these precious souls wonder why they allowed themselves to believe that God had somehow sanctioned their busyness.

Looking back, they wished they'd seen the warning signs. They say they'd give anything to go back and to have someone sit them down (like that precious woman did for me) and challenge their current pace and choices so they could have fixed the broken places in their wall.

Here's an important truth: When we run ourselves ragged doing too many things (most of which God never asked us to do), we leave unattended the sacred areas of our lives (e.g., intimacy with God, rich relationships with others, physical and spiritual health). What's the result? We miss out on the best of what God has for us, and we leave these areas exposed and vulnerable to the enemy's schemes. Read this important passage from Proverbs 25:28: "Like a city whose walls are broken through is a person who lacks self-control."

Think through that passage for a moment. A life without self-control leaves a person as vulnerable to destruction as a city whose protective walls are in shambles. When we think of self-control, our minds typically leap to overeating or overspending. But all too often, we manage our time like we manage our money—more goes out than what comes in. We don't realize how our busyness makes us less stable and more vulnerable.

Though God calls us to live full, abundant lives, He doesn't run us ragged or ask us to grind our gears to the point of breakdown. We can trust Him to know what's best for us. If we don't practice a measure of restraint when it comes to all of our time commitments, if we don't say no to continual and perpetual busyness, we'll say yes to it by default and leave ourselves vulnerable as a result. Our human nature and our culture are powerful forces that compel us to commit to more than God asks of us. At some point, we have to humbly embrace this truth about ourselves: *We all have our limits.*

Tim Chester writes:

> People do *not* feel stressed simply because they have a lot going on. Most of us enjoy doing lots of things. We only feel busy when we try to do *more than we can.* The problem is not expecting to do a lot, but expecting to do a little bit more than is possible. . . . So here's a foundational truth for what follows: *God does not expect me to do more than I can.* . . . If God doesn't expect me to do more than I can, the key question to ask ourselves is: *Why am I trying to do more than I can?*[2]

Why *are* we so quick to say yes when no, at times, might be the better answer? What do we hope to gain (or avoid) by giving away our time to so many different things? Someone once said, "If the devil can't make us bad, he'll make us busy." We all fall into the trap of overcommitment from time to time, but it's important to understand the cost every time we do.

Overcommitment puts a strain on our relationships, our physical health, and our ability to make sound decisions. When we give away our time to too many things at once, we also give away these precious things:

- Our times of refreshment (time freely spent in the Lord's presence to be strengthened, renewed, and redirected by Him)
- Our sense of well-being (margin that allows for rest, exercise, and time and space to spontaneously respond to the nudge of the Holy Spirit)
- Our perspective (the ability to view our lives through the lens of God's promises instead of our problems)

When we're in over our head, we tend to shift to a get-through-the-moment kind of mindset. We take costly shortcuts that we pay for later (more about this in the next chapter). When we run from one thing to the next, we miss the beauty and sacredness of the present moment, and we're less likely to identify where the enemy has set a trap for us. Sometimes we're the last ones to discern our own vulnerabilities. That's why we need to stand in the gap for each other like my new friend did for me.

About a year ago, I sent a letter to a pastor friend of mine. I took the risk and issued him the same caution my friend issued me. First I shared my experience with my friend, and then I wrote the following exhortation to him:

You have God-given leadership abilities, but you're worn out. You seem a little jaded by the ministry thing (I was there too), and you're physically tired. Your sweet wife is weary and needs you. Here's my charge to you, friend: Pull back and reignite your love affair and intimacy with

Jesus and with your wife, make time for your kids, and get back in shape physically.

Make everything else get in line and take a number. I promise you that if you seek first His kingdom and guard first your marriage, your family, and your physical health, you'll last long, finish strong, and be established in God's best for you.

God bless you, brother. I believe with all my heart that God wants to nourish, revive, and reset you in a way that feels wonderful to you and protects all that you love.

Kevin and I are seeing once-godly marriages drop like flies all around us. It's caused us to close the ranks on our own marriage even more and to be bolder when it comes to our friends. We're enjoying our marriage now more than we ever have. And we're stronger in ministry now more than ever. I do believe it's because of changes we made years ago.

I welcome your thoughts or any response you want to give me. I do hope you know that I come to you in brotherly love.

Thankfully, this friend responded just as I anticipated he would. He graciously thanked me for taking the risk to challenge him in this way, and he said it confirmed some of the things God had already been speaking to him. He made the necessary changes that were life-giving for him and his family.

Here's another important point: *We're not called to a busyness that drains us; we're called to an abundance that trains us.* Amidst our constant busyness, the enemy would love nothing more than for us to embrace a false sense of security. We tend to think that we've managed the craziness up to this point without any major mishaps, so we must be in better shape than most. But this is no way to live, and it's exactly the mindset the enemy wants us to have. Read these cautionary words from Beth Moore:

> We begin to see a few little hints of weakness in the boundary here and there, but with our busy lives we often pay little attention. Here's the big one: we reason that, after all, nothing disastrous has happened before. Listen carefully, never assume that just because a smaller problem hasn't exploded into a bigger problem before, it's never going to. Wrong. That's exactly what the enemy wants us to think. Don't ever forget what a schemer he is.[3]

In the pages ahead, we'll unearth some of the reasons for our constant and continual busyness. We'll look at the fear of others' opinions and even the ungodly sense of obligation that drives us to say yes when God would have us say no . . . all so we can say yes to something altogether different and better for us.

Not to say that God only invites us to do those things we love to do. Dying to ourselves that we might more boldly live for God is a painful (yet beautiful) process. Obeying Him when it doesn't suit us is downright hard. But every hard thing God asks us to do is always accompanied by His promise to transform us as we go. It's always an invitation to something more, something better than we would ever choose for ourselves.

Always and forever, we must remember that where He guides, He provides, what He asks of us, He supplies for us. No matter if He calls us up a mountain or down through the valley, He promises to stay by our side and to whisper in our ear, *"This is the way, walk ye in it."* He leads us on paths of righteousness for *His* namesake. Nothing compares to walking intimately and powerfully with God through every season of life.

Precious Lord,
    Lead me to the Rock that is higher than me. Give me
a renewed perspective of my life and of Your great love

for me. Show me even now which of my time commitments put me at risk and drain me of my precious energy. What are the next steps I should take, Lord? Show me the broken-down places in my wall—the areas of my life I've neglected because I've been too busy doing other things. Give me a fresh vision of Your best will for me in this particular season of life. What do You have for me here? What am I missing? What promises are mine for the taking?

I long to live in the ebb and flow of Your grace and goodness. Forgive me for my tendency to do more than You've asked of me. Forgive me for the countless times I allow my mind to wander to worry and angst. I will rest in Your presence today. I choose to embrace the truth of Your unfathomable love for me even when it's hard for me to believe it. I choose to see life as a precious gift straight from Your hand. I choose to remember that my yes and no are sacred and set apart for You, Lord. Fill me up to overflowing so that I may be a wellspring of life to everyone I meet. Thank You for new mercies and new beginnings. I trust You with my life and look forward to learning what it means to live out of Your divine supply for me. I love You, Lord. Amen.

Personal Reflection

1. What time commitments currently drain you?
2. Looking back, did you seek God's wisdom before you said yes to each of these commitments? (No condemnation here; just take them one by one.)
3. What's the cost of these commitments?
   a. Time-wise
   b. Emotionally
   c. Relationally
   d. Spiritually

4. What important things are you *not* tending to because of the time and space these commitments require? Honestly assess areas you've neglected. What parts of your life need attention?

5. What are some next steps the Lord would have you take to refortify your life in these areas (e.g., reprioritize prayer time with your spouse; stay off the Internet after everyone has gone to bed; plan for and prioritize exercise)?

A *Wise Word*

We would be better Christians if we spent more time alone, and *we would actually accomplish more if we attempted less and spent more time in isolation and quiet waiting upon God.* The world has become too much a part of us, and we are afflicted with the idea that we are not accomplishing anything unless we are always busily running back and forth. We no longer believe in the importance of a calm retreat where we sit silently by the shade. . . . [Yet] we can never have too many of these open spaces in life—hours set aside when our soul is completely open and accessible to any heavenly thought or influence that God may be pleased to send our way.[4]

Group Discussion Starters

1. Read the Wise Word quote above again. Consider what it means to have an "accessible" soul. How accessible are you regarding God's input in your life?
   a. Are there certain times of day when you're more apt to hear His voice?
   b. What times are you more likely to miss Him?

   c. Are there any adjustments you can make so you can better hear Him during those times of day?

2. Share about a time you committed to something for all of the wrong reasons. How did that go for you?

   a. What price did you pay?

   b. What did you learn?

3. Looking at your current time commitments, which commitment are you sure is God-ordained? How do you know?

4. What areas in your life do you sense God wants you to fortify and give more time to? What has to go so you can tend to this part of your "wall"?

Faith Declaration

I declare in the mighty name of Jesus that I am an anointed, appointed child of God! I am filled with the Holy Spirit and empowered by His love. I walk in the Lord's presence as I live here on earth. I have eyes to see, ears to hear, and a heart to do His will. I refuse to throw my yes around like it doesn't matter. Life is a gift, and my time is a gift. God invites me to walk with Him and do the next thing He gives me to do. I am loved, called, and fully equipped to live the powerful life God has assigned to me. I refuse the rat race because God has called me to the sacred race. And I will run with holy passion and conviction. In Jesus' name I pray, Amen!

✤ 2 ✤

When I Move Too Fast

Say Yes to God's Power

Cease striving and know that I am God; I will be exalted among the nations, I will be exalted in the earth.

Psalm 46:10 NASB

Though my work often consumed me, I was losing my pleasure in it—and for that matter, in many other things besides—and losing too, my effectiveness in it. And here's a secret: for all my busyness, I was increasingly slothful. . . . I was squandering time, not redeeming it.[1]

Mark Buchanan

Can you think of a time in your life (maybe you're in such a season right now) when, amidst all of your busyness, you sensed very little traction in it all? Isn't it something how during such times, that for all of our output, the only return on our investment seems to be soul weariness and mind fatigue? We might have scratched a few items from our task list, but have we *gained* the fresh wonder and godly anticipation that Jesus invites us to? More often than not, I'd say the answer is no. Wouldn't you? Yet with all of the life-demands begging for our attention, we often feel as though we cannot and must not slow down. We're more worried about letting everybody else down than we are about wearing ourselves down. But that ungodly sense of obligation does not come from above. In fact, the Lord invites us, even charges us, to *stop* all of our striving and know that He is God (see Psalm 46:10).

To strive is to strain through life as if it all depends upon us. It's the notion: If it's to be, it's up to me. To know that He is God is to listen for His voice and do what He says. We steward the gifts He puts in our hands and we embrace expectant faith that He will multiply our offering. To know Him this way is to know and love Him so well that we allow nothing to come between us.

When we know God intimately, we enjoy His presence, we trust His voice, and we understand on a deeper level why we need Him to direct our every step. In fact, Proverbs 9:10 reminds us that it's wise to have a healthy fear of God, And the more we get to know Him, the more deeply we'll understand Him: "The fear of the Lord is the beginning of wisdom, and knowledge of the Holy One is understanding." You know what I just love about this verse? It calls us to understand and remember that He is God Almighty, and we'd be wise to honor Him as such. Yet at the same time, it reminds us that we're invited to know Him deeply and intimately. Juxtaposed in the same verse are these two profound truths:

- He is our star-breathing God and deserves our honor and awe.
- He is our loving Savior and invites us to intimacy, to know Him well.

31

And what do we do with such an offer? We reject it—or at best, we squander it. We run to and fro through life and consider our time with God more of a draining obligation than a life-giving invitation.

So what do we miss out on when we move too fast? We miss the best, most sacred parts of life.

We pay a huge price when we run ourselves ragged. Last chapter we addressed some of the dangers of the frantic pace. This chapter I want to make the distinction between doing life at a sprint pace and tapping in to the power that God has made available to us in this life. We'll also explore God's invitation to actually live with a settledness in our spirit and a heart at rest.

Don't you long to be more intimately acquainted with the One who gives us the gift of life with every breath we take and every step we make? I do too.

"For in him we live and move and have our being." As some of your own poets have said, "We are his offspring."

Acts 17:28

Live in Response, Not Reaction

Every year, countless Christians burn out and fall out of the race due to exhaustion and soul weariness. Author and pastor Kevin DeYoung says that busyness kills more Christians each year than bullets.[2] We're most vulnerable when we're tired, stretched sorely thin, and left with little reserve. When we consistently move too fast, we become crisis managers, living more in reaction to the next thing than in response to our loving King.

When we move too fast, we make a habit of taking detrimental shortcuts, which over time cost us greatly. For example, when the *rule* rather than the exception becomes:

- Fast-food diets instead of healthy food
- Hasty credit card purchases instead of mindful budgeted purchases
- One-minute devotions instead of time camped in the presence of God
- Text or Facebook messages instead of phone calls or face-to-face times with loved ones
- Connecting more deeply with people at work than with our loved ones at home

When we run too hard, too fast, for too long, we lose our perspective, our joy, and our sense of being sacredly present in the moment—not to mention the impact to our health and our relationships.

Though it feels like we gain a little extra distance or traction in the moment when we pick up speed and keep our foot on the pedal for an extended period of time, in reality we lose ground when we live like this. When we try to run a marathon at sprint pace, we miss life, the life God intended for us, and we can't possibly savor the sacred sweet journey up mountains, through valleys, and by still waters.

In Genesis we read about how Esau gave up his birthright for a bowl of soup. He let himself get so exhausted, so extended, so hungry that he lost sight of the bigger story of his life. He traded his birthright—something that would impact future generations—for a bowl of soup. Soup! Yet that's exactly what we do when we extend ourselves to the point of exhaustion and reduce our choices to options that just get us through the moment.

When we live bound so tightly to this earth, we miss out on opportunities that can have eternal significance. We deprive future generations the blessings God promised us—things we are called to lay hold of and to pass on to the next generations—when our consistent goal becomes one of filling a temporary need because we're moving too fast to think long-term.

It's time to cease striving and stop the craziness. And the only way to do that is to start today by truly, deeply, profoundly knowing and believing that *He is God* and that more rests on His shoulders than on ours.

Read the passage below and consider this truth: Those who strive in their own strength, as a way of life, will miss the divine opportunities God offers them. It's far too easy to overemphasize our immediate wants and underestimate the eternal significance of the moment, especially when we move at breakneck speed. When we drive too hard, we put ourselves at risk of taking costly shortcuts that can have long-term implications.

> And Esau said to Jacob, I beg of you, let me have some of that red lentil stew to eat, for I am faint and famished! That is why his name was called Edom [red]. Jacob answered, Then sell me today your birthright (the rights of a firstborn). Esau said, See here, I am at the point of death; what good can this birthright do me? Jacob said, Swear to me today [that you are selling it to me]; and he swore to [Jacob] and sold him his birthright. Then Jacob gave Esau bread and stew of lentils, and he ate and drank and rose up and went his way. Thus Esau scorned his birthright as beneath his notice.
>
> Genesis 25:30–34 AMP

Like Esau, if we drive ourselves to the point of fatigue and exhaustion, we'll scorn our birthright as beneath our notice. We'll become so desperate for momentary relief that we'll forget who we are. When we miss the greater promise written over our lives, others miss out on something God intended to give them through us. Someone once said, "A thousand people wait on the other side of your obedience."

How do we redeem our moments and eternally invest them?

- We pray, "Lord, give me eyes to see, ears to hear, and a heart to do Your will."
- We refuse to run through our days without a sense of God's presence. We cultivate a lifestyle of prayer.
- We accept our limitations and dare to say no if God hasn't given us a yes.
- We tackle our everyday tasks with a heart of faith, trusting God to multiply our efforts and show us His heart for the things He's given us to do.
- We embrace an expectancy that as we abide in Him and steward what He gives, more will be given to us and through us when we're ready for it.

Un-appointed Busyness vs. God-Ordained Fruitfulness

So how do we discern the difference between un-appointed busyness and God-ordained fruitfulness? Jesus taught us to look at the fruit. Pause here for a moment and look over your shoulder at the busyness of this past year. Has all of your output left you with an increased sense of expectancy and wonder?

Have you seen God take your offering and multiply it in a way that is beyond you? Do you see your fruit bearing more fruit? For example, have you invested in someone's life who now invests in others? Have you given to a ministry that increasingly makes a difference in the lives of many?

Are you more convinced than ever that God means what He says when He says His promises are true *for you*? Based on what you've just seen God do in and through you, do you find your prayers growing more audacious and your vision for what's possible even greater still?

By the way, if you answered yes to any of these questions, pause and thank Him today! Stay the course. Trust His love. And do what He says. He'll guide your every step.

But maybe that's not been the case for you. Would you say that your efforts seemed more about the sprint to keep up with it all? And that looking back for you is very much like looking ahead? You simply wonder how long you can sustain this pace. If that's you, do not despair. I promise you, God has a more life-giving journey for you than the one you've been on. Refuse the condemnation the enemy throws your way and instead consider the invitation from God Himself: "You did not choose me, but I chose you and appointed you so that you might go and bear fruit—fruit that will last—and so that whatever you ask in my name the Father will give you" (John 15:16).

How do we know if we're driving too hard in a way that God never sanctioned? We pay attention to how our efforts impact us and those we love. Take a look at these life-draining motivations and see if any resonate with you:

- External pressure without internal conviction
- The need to impress
- The need to save face (to manage others' opinions of you)
- The need to gain acceptance
- Fear of rejection
- The need to fill a gap or role that God didn't ask you to fill
- The need to postpone conflict
- The need to compensate for shortcoming in another area of life

Amidst our personal inventory, here's an important thought to consider: God uses us even when we're a bit out of balance. He works through us even when we've shown up for the wrong reasons. Why? Because He loves us. He sees us as works in progress. And He loves this world that's very much in need. He works through us to meet our needs; we are His beloved children, His very dear friends.

I often marvel that God will use me on a Monday, knowing I'm about to blow it on Tuesday. He's not after perfection; He moves on faith. He'll take whatever offering we give Him and use it for His glory and for our greater good. I just love that about Him!

But here's the thing: We'll not see the abundance of fruit Jesus promised, nor will we be able to sustain a life of abundance, unless we're deeply connected to the Vine *as a way of life.*

Abundant life centers around God's saving and healing work in our lives. It's about His grace at work in us, through us, and all around us. Imagine yourself having the grace to live, give, and serve in ways above and beyond you, in a way that reflects God's generous and loving heart for the world! And imagine others rising up and thanking God because of how they've been blessed by Him through you. That's God's promise to us: "And God is able to bless you abundantly, so that in all things at all times, having all that you need, you will abound in every good work" (2 Corinthians 9:8).

As we walk intimately with God, we grow in our capacity to manage greater measures of His abundance. We notice a greater distinction between the ebb and flow to our lives. We'll recognize seasons and moments of great output, and seasons and moments to pull back and rest.

The beautiful thing about the ebb and flow of life with God is that we'll have grace to do both as He assigns. During great times of output, we'll learn how to strategically trim the fat off of our day so as to manage the "much" God has given us to do. And we won't judge those who don't seem to be working as hard as we are, because we'll understand that God's sacred path of obedience looks different on all of us.

And during the ebb seasons, where God pulls us back and calls us to regroup and reset, we'll have the sense to follow Him there. We'll refuse the temptation to feel insecure for doing less because we'll come to appreciate that rest is as much a discipline as work is, and we'll entrust our identity and our fruitfulness to Jesus.

As God's beloved, redeemed ones, He invites us to join Him as He moves on the earth so that we might live with eternity in mind. How we live here impacts how we live in heaven, where we'll be forever with Him. What we possess of His promises now impacts what we possess of them then, when Jesus comes for His Church.

When we reach for all God offers us, we find we have too much to keep for ourselves. With every healing step we take, we gain passion for those who need what God has made available to us all. As we find wholeness and strength in Him, we can't help but point others to Jesus.

The more intimately we walk with God, the more clearly we see ourselves as conduits of His kingdom, vessels of His love, branches deeply connected to the Vine. Fruit begins to abound from our lives, leaving others nourished and strengthened because of who God is, in and through us. When we live in such close communion with God that His life flows freely through our life, we leave people and places better than we found them, just like Jesus did.

The more we discern what Jesus offers to this lost and dying world, the more He's able to entrust us with the treasures of His kingdom, because we'll dare to believe Him for the "more" He offers. This kind of abundance changes us from the inside out. We learn to trust God more than we trust ourselves. We rely more on His greatness than we do on our own commandment-keeping goodness. Though we see the importance of wisely stewarding our gifts and abilities, we know that it's God's power alone that makes things grow (see 1 Corinthians 3:7).

Our souls find rest and our lives bear fruit when we abide in Christ. Indeed, it's in our close communion with the Lord that we learn how much more rests on His shoulders than on ours. And as we learn to abide, we take our rest cues and our work cues from above. We more quickly discern our tendency to strive and make the necessary corrections before too much time passes. We pay attention to the warning signs God puts in our path because we're teachable and humble and expectant.

Like those in recovery from addiction, we admit our utter dependency on God, and we know to be especially careful when we're hungry, angry, lonely, and tired. We guard our hearts and our lives, and we view our steps as sacred because we are set apart by God Himself. Jesus told us the enemy's focus and passion is to destroy everything good in our lives. But thankfully, Jesus came to save, restore, and renew us beyond what we ever thought possible.

> The thief does not come except to steal, and to kill, and to destroy. I have come that they may have life, and that they may have it more abundantly,
>
> John 10:10 NKJV

Jesus intends to fill us with His abundance, to use us in profound ways on this journey, and to lead us safely home.

Precious Lord,
Thank You for the countless ways You've protected me when I was most vulnerable and unaware of the enemy's access to me. Thank You for Your constant patience and grace during those times I've strived in my own strength. Forgive me for how forgetful I can be! Take me to the higher road You have for me. Help me to see life from Your point of view. Let me not miss the sacred and eternal moments You've put before me. Fill me up to overflowing. Give me eyes to see and ears to hear and a heart to do Your will. I

*long to know You more! I don't want to race through this
life and miss the very reason You've placed me here for such
a time as this. Make Your Word come alive in me. Give me
Your divine strategy for a life of rhythm and grace. I want
to have the courage to run when You tell me to run and to
rest when You tell me to rest. You know me best and love
me most. I will follow You forever. I am Yours and You are
mine. Change me from the inside out. I want my life to count
for all eternity. Thank you, God, for Your never-ending
faithfulness to me. My soul rests secure in You. Amen.*

Personal Reflection

1. Is there an area of your life where you operate as if more
   rests on your shoulders than on God's? Pause and pray. Ask
   God to show you His heart for you, especially regarding
   this particular area of your life.
   a. Invite Him to renew your thoughts in a way that changes
   your approach to this area of your life. (He'll gladly
   do this for you.)
2. Think about your pace over the past week or so. Do you
   have a greater sense of God's rhythm for you, or do you
   still feel stuck in a sprint pace? Explain.
3. Amidst the busyness of your life, can you identify some
   moments of grace—moments where you scooped up your
   everyday duties and offered them to the Lord?
4. Ask the Lord to show you a time this past week when you
   missed His best will for you. Can you think of a moment
   when He invited you to rest and you decided to strive? Or
   He invited you to give to someone else and you decided
   to indulge yourself? Without any condemnation, ask His
   forgiveness and then receive the forgiveness He freely offers. Ask Him for an increased awareness of His voice
   and direction in your life.

5. One of the enemy's most-used weapons against us is our "not-enough-ness"—we don't give enough, pray enough, serve enough, and love enough. Yet in all of our lack, we're still exhausted from doing too much. This is the cycle he hopes to use to hold us captive. But it's for freedom that Christ has set us free! How do you deal with the enemy's harassment? Does it get the best of you? Are you held captive by this lie? Or are you able to put him under your feet? Explain.

A *Wise Word*

The more we are strengthened by the Holy Spirit, the more we will be like the Lord Jesus Himself. And the more we are like Him, the more He will "settle down and feel completely at home in our hearts." We enter into the enjoyment of His indwelling through faith. This involves constant dependence on Him, constant surrender to Him, and constant recognition of His "at home-ness." It is through faith that we 'practice the presence His presence' as Brother Lawrence quaintly put it.[3]

Instead of allowing the enemy's constant not-enough-ness message to settle into your soul, wrap your arms around the idea that *Christ in you is your hope of glory.* Allow His "at-home-ness" to trump your not-enough-ness every single day of the week.

Group Discussion Starters

1. Talk about the difference between a busyness that drains us and an abundance that trains us. Why do you suppose certain people can manage the "much" God has given them to do and still manage a healthy rhythm and right relationship with God?

2. When you consider your current stage of life, in what areas do you find yourself slipping into that striving mode and forgetting to engage your faith?

3. If you know someone who lives out of that abiding, abundant place with God, what challenges and inspires you about his or her life?

4. Are you more apt to overcommit and run yourself ragged, or do you tend to self-preserve in a way that keeps you from the adventure of faith?

5. What does a healthy balance look like for you in this stage of life?

Faith Declaration

I declare in the mighty name of Jesus that I am an anointed, appointed child of God! I am filled with the Holy Spirit and empowered by His love. I walk in the Lord's presence as I live here on earth. I have eyes to see, ears to hear, and a heart to do His will. I refuse to throw my yes around like it doesn't matter. Life is a gift, and my time is a gift. God invites me to walk with Him and do the next thing He gives me to do. I am loved, called, and fully equipped to live the powerful life God has assigned to me. I refuse the rat race because God has called me to the sacred race. And I will run with holy passion and conviction. In Jesus' name I pray, Amen!

✤ 3 ✤

Busyness vs. Abundance

Say Yes to God's Provision

I am the vine; you are the branches. If you remain in me and I in you, you will bear much fruit; apart from me you can do nothing.

John 15:5

I've noticed that when people start to live every day in active cooperation with the Spirit, something astonishing happens: they immediately recognize the life God intended for them.[1]

Bruce Wilkinson

She approached me like she knew me well. I'd maybe seen her a time or two. I smiled and greeted her. Without further ado she shared her perspective of my life with me: "I've been watching you from a distance, and I've told people, 'She's going to crash and burn. Just watch, she's going to wake up one day and not be able to get out of bed.' With all you do, it's impossible to keep it up. You're just going to burn out one day and not be able to move."

Not exactly an encouraging conversation.

Though I didn't need to explain my life or schedule to her, I wanted to. So I touched her arm, thanked her for her concern, and proceeded to explain some of the safeguards I've put in my life—disciplines that hem me in and hold me up. At the end of our conversation, she replied by saying something like, "Wow, *I* don't even do those things. I had no idea. I just watch you from a distance and think there's no way possible for one person to accomplish so much. I tried to picture doing what you do and assumed that if it would kill me, it'd probably kill you too. I just figured you were doing too much."

Sobering words, no? The thing is, both my husband and I *do* manage a lot. But we didn't get to this place overnight. For years God has trained us and refined us, corrected us and redirected us, strengthened us and established us. Since we've earnestly and consistently asked Him to do so, He's been teaching us to live focused, faith-filled lives. Still, we are very much works in progress.

We've stepped back from certain commitments and stepped up to others. We've seen firsthand how far more fruitful we are now than we were back then—now that we purposefully stay closely connected to the Lord and to each other. Here in this place, Kevin and I accomplish five times more than when we almost crashed and burned. Granted, we're older, wiser, and empty nesters, but we are thriving in the process.

We enjoy life. We laugh a lot, we play with our dog, we watch movies, and we get to bed at a decent time every night. So how is this season in our lives different from the one fifteen years ago? Let's look again at Jesus' words to us in the gospel of John: "I am the vine; you are the branches. If you remain in me and I in you, you will bear *much fruit*; apart from me you can do nothing" (John 15:5).

Years ago, when we headed down the road to burnout, we ran parallel paths; we sacrificed our relationships, especially with each other. Mixed in with our God-given assignments were commitments we made without consulting God. We served at church—that was a given. But back then, when we saw additional needs, we stepped up beyond what God had asked us to. Guess what? The need doesn't always dictate the call. We learned that the hard way.

It's true, all those years ago, my husband and I had immersed ourselves in busyness and overcommitment, and it almost killed us. Praise God for His intervention in our lives. Part of our recovery involved establishing clear boundaries around our time and prioritizing the life-giving yeses God invited us to engage in. As an example, in addition to our individual morning devotional times, Kevin and I pray together every morning and every night.

That one daily discipline has revolutionized our lives. We guard our bedtime so we get enough sleep. We intentionally challenge ourselves to increase our giving every year not only to our local church but to kingdom ministries that God directs us to sow into.

Personally, I engage in several disciplines that help me with some of the health challenges I still deal with. I work out several times a week. I drink about sixty ounces of water a day. I eat healthy food and enjoy an occasional sweet treat. I stretch every day. You get the idea. These strategies strengthen me and enable me to carry more at age fifty than I ever carried at age thirty.

We've guarded these disciplines because we see how fruitful and life-giving they are to us. While some have critiqued how we've guarded those boundaries, others have critiqued how much we give away. Everyone has opinions about how you and I live. But they won't be the ones standing with us on judgment day when we're asked to give an account for how we stewarded the life God offered us. We will face God on our own.

That's why—though it's important to remain humble, teachable, and open to correction—it's vitally important to take our cues from the Lord and to *live* for Him, for an audience of One. The more you and I entrust our yeses and no's to the Savior, the more people will have opinions about how we live. I'm not sure why certain people have such strong opinions about why we do the things we do, but they will and they do. When we embrace a God-given vision and employ the disciplines He sets out for us, some may think us too legalistic. When we feel the strong call not to make a move but to wait on God, some may think us too passive. When we encounter the questions and assessments of others, you and I can graciously share our hearts in the best way we know how. And some will get it, but others won't. That's okay. Stay kind. Stay gentle. But stay the course. Bruce Wilkinson writes:

> For a personal miracle, you must choose to proactively partner with God's supernatural power to do what no good work of your own could. All of Christ's followers have been invited into this amazing partnership with Heaven. It's a joint but unequal venture between weak humans and an extraordinary God to pursue His agenda in His way in His time by His power and for His glory. This amazing partnership changes what we do, how we think, and what we know is possible.[2]

Life-Giving Boundaries—a Framework for the Impossible

Kevin and I have found that these personal boundaries don't make us selfish and self-focused. In fact, for us, it's been just the opposite. During our prayer times, God has burdened our hearts for the world, for human trafficking victims, for the poor and the orphaned. More recently, He has stirred our hearts for our city and for the ministries that reach out to the least of these. Our kingdom influence in the world has grown exponentially from that small, hidden, abiding place of prayer. And as we've seen God move on our prayers, we've developed an appetite for the impossible.

> If you live in me and what I say lives in you, then ask for anything you want, and it will be yours. You give glory to my Father when you produce a lot of fruit and therefore show that you are my disciples.
>
> John 15:7–8 GW

Years ago we asked God to do in and *through us* the above-and-beyond-all-we-could-ever-dare-to-ask-or-think. We asked for an abundantly increased anointing on our lives. In other words, we asked Him to empower us to live lives totally disproportionate to who we are so that when others see the fruit and the life that come from us, they'll be inspired to look up and trust God for *themselves*. We're excited to think of the kingdom impact of countless believers praying and giving of themselves and their resources audaciously.

Those who know us closely know how we live and what we prioritize. And they have permission and invitation to speak into our lives whenever they feel the need. We believe accountability provides safety.

Still, We Get Weary

But just because we live by faith and trust God in bold and audacious ways doesn't mean we won't have times where we feel weary or overwhelmed. We do have those days, and we take them as our cue that it's time to get some added rest. Weariness is not a disqualifier or even an indicator that we're out of God's will. Even Jesus got weary on occasion.

I've had both Caroline and Matthew Barnett on my radio show several times. They manage the mind-boggling ministry of The Dream Center in Los Angeles, California. They feed and care for thousands of people. They live lives utterly disproportionate to who they are. Talk about a life of abundance! I asked Caroline if she gets discouraged when she gets tired. Here's what she said:

> It's easy to get overwhelmed, but it's just as easy to rest in God. When you find yourself feeling discouraged in your service to others, tired from the hard work your ministry requires, or stressed from trying to juggle a life of service with a personal life . . . just take a break. Take five minutes out of your day and find a quiet place to get back into the presence of God.[3]

There's nothing like a Sabbath moment to reset our perspective!

If we serve God and believe Him for big things, we'll have lots to do in a day. Dr. Mark Rutland said it best the last time he was on my show: "We ask God to bless our work and we want Him to establish the work of His hands. But you know what happens when He blesses our work, don't you? He gives us more work to do. And we are grateful." Perfectly said.

When we give God our yes and we walk by faith, God will do the impossible in and through us. And those who know us best and love us most will encourage us when we're weary.

However, we may also excite the jealousies or the critiques of others who watch us from a distance. The fear of man tends to creep in and tempts us to dim our light so that others won't oppose or unfairly assess us.

Oftentimes people question or wrongly assess us because they're projecting how our assignment might impact them. But they're not the ones suited to carry it. We are. And God has been conditioning you and me every day, every step of the way. It's easy to be the critic. It takes courage to stay so fixed on God's will that you follow Him anyway. Say yes anyway. God will cover you and defend you.

Busyness or Abundance?

Look amongst your fellow Christ followers. Pay attention to how they do life. See if you notice a difference between those who live abundantly full lives (fruit-full, joy-full, faith-filled lives) and those who live busy lives (rushing, racing, stressing lives). More often than not, you'll notice one of them has a countenance of peace and joy, expectancy and humility, and even perhaps surprise sometimes because of God's divine movement.

The other—more often than not—wears a countenance that reveals strain and fatigue, weariness and frustration, and even disillusionment sometimes because of the seeming lack of power in his or her life.

You may find these people on the same committees at church or in the same pew on Sundays. But the places they serve *from* are worlds apart.

There are those who tap in to God Himself for their strength. They prioritize, spending time in His presence. They daily cultivate a lifestyle of dependency on Him, receive their marching orders from Him, and entrust their offerings to Him. On one hand they know their limits, but on the other, their lives seem to bear fruit that goes above and beyond their gifts and abilities. They understand that they are vessels God delights to fill and spill,[4] and they live out of the divine supply God offers them.

Other men and women rush from one thing to the next. Though they rise early and go to bed late, there seems to be no end to their task lists and no time for them to meet with

God. They strive in their own strength, feel the constant strain of their limitations, and wonder why others don't step up so they won't have to do so much. They long for a better way to live but don't know how to get there from here.

God loves all of these men and women dearly and deeply. But *only one* of these lifestyles is sustainable. Jesus intends for us to live abundant, fruitful, faith-filled lives, and the only way this is possible is through our loving, intimate connection with Him. He's the Source, the very Vine of life. We are the branches. We draw life from Him, for Him, with Him, so we can be much through Him. Apart from Him we can do nothing of substance, nothing that lasts.

> Remain in me, as I also remain in you. No branch can bear fruit by itself; it must remain in the vine. Neither can you bear fruit unless you remain in me. I am the vine; you are the branches. If you remain in me and I in you, you will bear much fruit; apart from me you can do nothing. If you do not remain in me, you are like a branch that is thrown away and withers; such branches are picked up, thrown into the fire and burned. If you remain in me and my words remain in you, ask whatever you wish, and it will be done for you. This is to my Father's glory, that you bear much fruit, showing yourselves to be my disciples.
>
> John 15:4–8

It's a beautiful day when we realize that apart from Christ, we can do nothing. What a relief! Deep inside, most of us know we have only so much to offer. But when we understand that in Christ we're able to live out of His abundance, we learn to prioritize and cultivate a rich devotional life. We unapologetically make time for rest and replenishment. We come to believe in the power of prayer and the promise of seeds sown. We learn to trust God more than we trust ourselves. And we learn to cultivate a sense of His presence as we live here on earth (see Psalm 116:9).

Precious Lord,

I open my hands and receive all that You have for me this day! I refuse to acknowledge or listen to the condemnation the enemy throws my way. Instead, I embrace Your mercy and grace, which allow me to be a work in progress.

Forgive me for straining and striving through life when You've called me to an abiding and thriving kind of life. You've awakened my heart to believe You for the impossible, and so I say, Here I am, Lord. Fill me, spill me, correct me, redirect me. Make me new and renew my heart for You. I want the kind of life You dreamed up for me when You first had the idea of me. I want my life to bear such incredible fruit that others come to know and believe that You are God—full of power, fully at work in the world today! Do the impossible in and through me, Lord. Show me what has to go so I can lay hold of more of You. You're everything to me, Lord. And I'm everything to You. How blessed I am to be known so intimately by You. Lead me in Your everlasting way. I will follow You, one grace-step at a time. Amen.

Personal Reflection

1. Dream with me for a moment. If you imagined your life to be above and beyond all you could ever dare to ask or think according to Christ's glorious work in and through you (see Ephesians 3:20–21), what would that abundant life look like on you?

2. Is it more instinctive for you to strive in your own strength or to seek first God's order of things? How did you get to this place?

3. Sometimes we can clearly see God's hand of blessing in one area of our lives, but not so much in another. Which

areas of life do you see God's favor? In which areas of life do you tend to struggle more than thrive? Why do you think that is?

4. Sometimes God simply allows seasons of barrenness before He brings the fruitfulness. At other times, our own striving may be a factor. Which is it for you? Do you sense God is training you to have faith in this area of struggle? Or do you admit that maybe you've taken matters into your own hands and need to release them back to God so you can do what He says?

5. What's God saying to you about the life of abundance He has for you? Write it down.

A Wise Word

God has a blueprint for every life. Before our conversion He mapped out a spiritual career for us. Our responsibility is to find His will for us and then obey it. We do not have to work out a plan for our lives, but only accept the plan that He has drawn up for us. This delivers us from fret and frenzy, and insures that our lives will be of maximum glory to Him, of most blessing to others, and of greatest reward to ourselves.[5]

Group Discussion Starters

1. Share about a time you felt pruned by God (where He cut back your activity, opportunity, ability, etc.) and what came out of that time.

2. Share about a time or a season when you felt especially close to the Lord. What were the circumstances that contributed to that experience?

3. How often do you take Sabbath moments to reset your perspective? What practical steps can you take in your current season of life to create a moment of replenishment in your day?

4. To say yes to God's abundance, we have to be willing to say no to over-busyness. What area(s) of your life needs reining in? Explain.

5. In what area of life do you want to see God's power at work?

Faith Declaration

I declare in the mighty name of Jesus that I am an anointed, appointed child of God! I am filled with the Holy Spirit and empowered by His love. I walk in the Lord's presence as I live here on earth. I have eyes to see, ears to hear, and a heart to do His will. I refuse to throw my yes around like it doesn't matter. Life is a gift, and my time is a gift. God invites me to walk with Him and do the next thing He gives me to do. I am loved, called, and fully equipped to live the powerful life God has assigned to me. I refuse the rat race because God has called me to the sacred race. And I will run with holy passion and conviction. In Jesus' name I pray, Amen!

4

There's Rest in God's Yes

Say Yes to God's Invitation

Are you tired? Worn out? Burned out on religion?
Come to me. Get away with me and you'll recover
your life. I'll show you how to take a real rest.
Walk with me and work with me—watch how
I do it. Learn the unforced rhythms of grace. I
won't lay anything heavy or ill-fitting on you. Keep
company with me and you'll learn to live freely
and lightly.

Matthew 11:28–30 MSG

I find that when I am most hurried, I run past much
that God is trying to show me, give me, lead me
into. . . . If we are followers of an unhurried Savior,
what should the pace of life look like?[1]

Alan Fadling

The coach pulled Leah aside, put his hands on his hips, and said, "You have more power in those legs than I've ever seen on a cyclist, but I can't train you—in fact, I *won't* train you—if you won't listen to me. You show up to practice as if every training day is a race day. You blow past every other cyclist like your only goal is to finish before they do. Don't you know they each have different goals for their specific training days? And if you'd listen to me, you'd know that some days I want you to ride with all of your might, but other days I just want you to flush out your legs. Some days I want you to work on improving your speed, and other days your strength.

"And another thing, even though you're filled with incredible muscle power and endurance, you'll *never* reach your potential by treating every moment as a sprint. Those who learn the secret of momentum are the ones who actually finish with a better race time. They train in a way that's sustainable over the long haul. They even recover from drills and races more easily than those who go all-out with no sense of restraint or discipline.

"If you're willing to listen to me, learn from me, and do what I say when I say it—if you're able to see that pulling back is as much a discipline as pushing forward—I can turn you into a powerful, professional cyclist."

Leah came to cycle class that day with a whole new lesson to teach us: *the power of momentum.* For the rest of the hour we practiced very distinct cycle patterns, ones that we'd dedicate whole classes to in the days to come.

One moment we all hunkered down and moved our legs so fast the studio practically shook. The next moment, we sat upright, kept our pedals moving, took a drink of water, a few deep breaths, and toweled ourselves off. One moment we cranked up the tension and slowly and steadily climbed a grueling hill. The next moment, we grabbed our handlebars, leaned over them, and pedaled uphill with high resistance as fast as we were able. Let me tell you, that's really hard.

Each of these drills accomplished something in us and for us. We dedicated whole classes to speed, strength, stamina, *and recovery*. In not very much time, most of us noticed significant gains in our fitness levels. Amazing what a few tweaks to a routine will do!

And guess what? My friend listened to her coach, did what he said, and in a matter of time, she became a professional cyclist—one who makes a habit of finishing on the platform with a medal around her neck.

Can you see the application here? If we approach every day the same way, like it's a sprint, we'll burn out and never reach our fullest potential. We need to develop a distinction between our hill-climbing days, our sprint days, and our recovery days. Just as the rhythm of Jesus' life had an ebb and flow, so must our lives.

And though we may feel we have no choice in how our days unfold, we actually can decide how we'll show up from day to day and when we'll steal away for a moment of soul-refreshment. To some degree, we take our cues from our body, our season of life, and our capacity at the moment.

But there's also an element of discipline and drive required, even for our moments and days of rest. Sometimes we almost have to "take sides against ourselves" and do what's best for us, whether we like it or not.

Allow me to make one more application here: Though each of us is on a pilgrimage to the Promised Land, we're all in different seasons and phases of this journey. God is working on one thing in you and another in me. You might be in recovery while I'm sprinting up a hill with heavy tension. We need to give one another permission to experience variations in the journey. We're not racing against each other. Comparing our performances makes no sense when you really think about it. Doing so can create unnecessary friction, jealousy, and disappointment.

We're all works in progress, in varying seasons of life. Discipline and application look different on each of us because our stories are unfolding in very different ways. Our experiences may overlap somewhat, but they impact us in a very personal way because we are *each* uniquely, fearfully, and wonderfully made.

Our bruises, our battles, and our dreams are all unique to us. Where you need work and where I need work are most likely worlds apart. And God, in His sovereign wisdom, masterfully considers our life season, our current obstacles, our hidden weaknesses and obvious strengths, and He leads us through an obstacle course that trains *us* for the course ahead of us. He teaches us how to triumph in spite of the enemy's efforts to trip us up.

If comparison or competition drives us through our days, we'll run ourselves ragged for all the wrong reasons and be miserable in the process.

It's strong, wise people who take their cues from Jesus because they know that He knows how to lead them, train them, and teach them in a way that prepares them for the road ahead.

He's hugely invested in our lives, and this is how He leads us:

- He leads us by still waters when our soul needs refreshment (Psalm 23).
- He trains our hands for battle so we're not pummeled by our enemy (Psalm 18).
- He teaches us to stand on high places and makes us spiritually agile (Psalm 18).
- He tucks us in the shadow of His wing so we can rest (Psalm 91).
- He teaches us to trust Him more than we trust ourselves (Proverbs 3).
- He takes responsibility to save us, defend us, and honor us (Psalm 62).

Scripture calls us to run the race to win the prize, which translates into call to be teachable, trainable, and focused. It's a call to live like we're participants, not spectators. It's a challenge to take our cues *from God*, not from the ridiculous pace of culture, or from the drive to compete or compare, and definitely not from the compulsion to dig ourselves out of an identity hole. We are beloved heirs of God with access to the provision of heaven. This race is an invitation to see what's possible when we take Him at His Word—and in His Word, He invites us, calls us, commands us, even, to rest.

> Then, because so many people were coming and going that they did not even have a chance to eat, he said to them, "Come with me by yourselves to a quiet place and get some rest."
>
> Mark 6:31

Come Away and Rest Awhile . . .

Picture yourself sitting under a giant oak tree, nestled in thick green grass. You look across the lake and marvel at the stillness of the water. You take a deep breath in and slowly exhale. You feel your nerves untwist and your soul unwind. You lean your head back against the tree and close your eyes. The winds gently blow, the trees clap their hands, and the birds sing an untethered song. Freedom. Rest. Replenishment. *Thank you, Jesus,* your soul whispers.

You open your eyes to find Jesus sitting next to you. With His forearms on His knees, He looks at you with a smile that goes all the way up to His eyes. With tender sincerity He says, *"I've been waiting for you."* You tilt your head and ask, "Waiting for *me*? Why?"

Why would Jesus *invite us* to come away and rest awhile? Why did He make it a regular practice Himself? Jesus treasured times with the Father because that's when His soul found rest and replenishment. It's when He connected with His Father. He wants that for us because He knows what it'll do for us. He knows how much our souls need a regular, intimate connection with the Father.

> Very early in the morning, while it was still dark, Jesus got up, left the house and went off to a solitary place, where he prayed.
>
> Mark 1:35

> After leaving them, he went up on a mountainside to pray. Later that night, the boat was in the middle of the lake, and he was alone on land.
>
> Mark 6:46–47

> Jesus gave them this answer: "Very truly I tell you, the Son can do nothing by himself; he can do only what he sees his Father doing, because whatever the Father does the Son also does. For the Father loves the Son and shows him all he does. Yes, and he will show him even greater works than these, so that you will be amazed."
>
> John 5:19–20

Let's consider our own life rhythm in light of what Jesus modeled for us. He unapologetically took time to get away to rest His soul and to be with the Father. Author Alan Fadling encourages us to believe that what was possible for Jesus is possible for us too.

> Jesus' pattern here is not superhuman. We can actually follow His example. If we feel we're too busy to follow Jesus in this way, perhaps we have made ourselves too busy. Jesus came to show us what a deeply rooted relationship of communion with the Father could look like, and I believe that the depth of His roots in this vital and divine relationship is one reason for the broad reach of His influence and for the fruitfulness of His life and ministry.[2]

As a whole, our motivated, driven, type-A culture tends to believe that if we do more, we'll produce more. But as we read in the gospel of John chapter 15, we find that we actually produce more by *being more* with Christ. "I am the vine; you are the branches. If you *remain in me* and I in you, you will bear *much fruit*; apart from me you can do nothing" (John 15:5, emphasis mine). Take a look at these descriptive words for *remain*:

- Continue
- Persist
- Stay
- Rest

Though we don't typically connect *effort* to rest, these words imply continual action and intention to remain in intimate fellowship with the Father.

And look at these descriptive words for *much*:

- A lot
- A great deal
- Very much
- A large, indefinite quantity

Here's a truth that will change our lives if we'll grasp it: When it comes to fruit borne out of our abiding place of rest with God, *continual, intentional remaining with Christ produces large quantities of fruit and a life of abundance. Abiding has an abundant, accumulative, beautiful effect on our lives.*

Think of how the currents of life tend to pull us away from our fellowship with God. Jesus had countless people pulling on Him. Still, He got away and rested in His Father's presence. He knew that *this* was the secret of replenishment and renewal, abundant fruit and eternal influence.

Jesus lived and breathed out of His intimate connection with the Father, and as a result, He was always in the right place at the right time so He could do and be and say and pray and live and give the way the Father wanted Him to. Jesus cultivated a continual-consistent-steady-remaining relationship with the Father. And every twist and turn of His life was anointed and appointed by God Himself.

When we follow the Savior, we can be assured that in God's yes, there'll always be an element of rest. He'll always provide still waters or streams in the desert when we need them. But if we don't see replenishment as a priority, we won't look for God's provisions along the way. Just as you see exit ramps to rest stops on a long road trip, God provides exit ramps to moments that will refill you on your journey.

Jesus is our lifeline, our very Source of life. We spend time with Him because nothing compares to having an intimate relationship with our Creator. Any gift from His hand pales in comparison to the treasure of knowing His heart. Time with God restores and revives our soul. Jesus is the greatest gift.

Yet the beautiful thing is, He gives us good gifts because that's how He is. That's who He is. He loves us deeply.

> The Lord is my shepherd, I lack nothing. He makes me lie down in green pastures, he leads me beside quiet waters, he refreshes my soul. He guides me along the right paths for his name's sake.
>
> Psalm 23:1–3

In Every Detail, Every Minute . . .

One of my closest friends is walking through a really tough valley right now. Her heart is broken. She's waited a long time for her breakthrough, and yet she's gotten good at noticing the still-water moments that Jesus continues to provide for her in the meantime. She spends regular times with her Lord, and as silly as it may sound to some, during one of their moments together, He nudged her to make a hair appointment. He cares about such things, you know.

> The Lord directs the steps of the godly. He delights in every detail of their lives.
>
> Psalm 37:23 NLT

My friend texted me today: "I went and got my hair done this morning. It felt so good. Was a gift from God." She's right. Every good gift comes from Him. He leads, He guides, He nourishes, He provides. He gives us those fill-me-back-up moments when we need them most.

You know what gives me rest and fills me back up again?

- Long quiet times of prayer and time in the Word
- Intense exercise
- Sitting by the lake and watching the sun set
- Times of prayer with my husband
- Snuggling with my pit bull
- Looking up at the sky and letting the sun warm my face while counting my blessings out loud
- Lighting a candle and sitting down to read a book

All of these moments refresh me because they compel me to pause, pray, look up, and remember that more rests on God's shoulders than on mine. And at least for me, the discipline of rest is as much an act of faith as hard work is. How about you? What nourishes your soul and compels you to find rest in God alone?

Since Jesus places a high priority on rest, you can know that you've got exit ramps all along your journey. Look for them.

They're invitations and provisions directly from Him. He knows what will fill your soul, and He invites you to rest in Him, to catch your breath, to find direction, and to gain a fresh perspective when you need one.

Dallas Willard once gave this advice to John Ortberg: "You must arrange your day so that you are experiencing deep contentment, joy, and confidence in your everyday life with God."[3]

What would need to change in your life—how do you need to rearrange your day—so you can experience regular deep contentment, joy, and confidence with God? Pause and really think about that question for a moment because it's a life-changing proposition.

Consider how we often approach life. We race ahead, caught up in this whac-a-mole culture, and we ask God to bless us quick: *"I need a green light here, Lord. I'm late!"* or, *"Please, please don't let that officer pull me over,"* or, *"Why did I sign up for this? How did I get myself into this mess? Lord, get me out!"* We race ahead and repeatedly beg God to bail us out.

It's like going on a long trip without making a plan. We find ourselves on an endless stretch of highway in the middle of nowhere with a gas tank that's about to run dry. Not to say that God won't provide a friendly stranger to give us a ride to the local gas station fifty miles away, but was this God's best plan for us in this particular part of the journey?

Here's an important point: God's love never goes away. Our mess-ups don't make Him give up on us. He'll meet us in all of our wandering ways and provide a way out and back to the path that's best for us. He provides new mercies every morning because we need them. But still, when we're sloppy with our yes, we miss out on God's best.

Now consider the invitation *not* to race ahead, but to follow God's leading in our lives. Go back to that spot by the tree, next to Jesus. Ask Him what you need to know for the road ahead. Give Jesus the opportunity to speak life to your soul. Let Him remind you how much He loves you and that nothing will ever separate you from His love or from the promise of His presence. Hand him your bag of worries, and He'll wrap you up in a blanket of strength and peace. Already you feel better. You're more assured than you were a moment ago. You know you'll be okay because you remember once again that He's always with you.

God points north and says, "Take that road. That's the one I want you on. Pack some snacks; in fact, take extra for the man on the side of the road. Keep your eyes open for him. Share what you have with him. Remember, don't panic when it rains. Just take it slow. There's a rest stop just outside of town. I've gone ahead and booked you a room. You'll know it when you see it. Stop there and rest. I'll tell you where to go from there."

Sometimes God gives us more information than we expect, and other times, less. But the point is, when we wait on Him, we stay in step with Him. And every step we take will have redemptive possibilities.

Author Bo Stern has been on my show a few times. She's a godly, beautiful example of a woman who abides deeply with God. She has a sign hanging in her office that reads: EVERY MINUTE. When her husband was diagnosed with ALS and given three to five years to live, she went facedown to the floor and (as she said) cried an ugly cry.

With her face in the carpet she sobbed for all she was about to lose. The enemy pressed in and said, "You're about to lose *everything*. Your husband is going to die and you'll be a widow. Your kids will lose their faith because of what God allows in your life. And you'll be alone and miserable." Underneath it all, in the depths of her being, in spite of her pain and fear, she continually heard the words, "Every minute. Every minute. Every minute."

She knew that voice well because she spends plenty of time in God's presence. She sat up and said, "Every minute, Lord? What does that mean?" The Lord broke through her pain and the enemy's spewing threats and proclaimed to her, "I've gone ahead of you and made a way for you. I've been to *every minute* you will ever face, and I've left provision for you there. Trust me. I am with you and will never forsake you."

Bo's story took my breath away. God continues to be faithful to this precious family. Men come regularly to the house to learn from Bo's husband because he's so deeply in tune with God's voice in this place. Bo loves Sunday nights best because her kids come home for Sunday night dinners and impromptu dance parties.

Everywhere she turns she finds God faithful to His Word. He's proven time and time again that He's been to every minute she'll ever face and left provision for her there. And He's done the same for you. You can afford to rest. In fact, you can't afford not to rest.

God intends for you to live out your days much like the ocean tide. In Him you'll find ebb and flow, a sacred rhythm that's life-giving and sustainable *for you*. Do what He says, and you'll become your best self.

He doesn't sanction or dictate an all-out sprint as a way of life. His ways for you are better than your ways. His thoughts toward you are higher than your own thoughts about yourself. His will for you is your best-case scenario. Be much with God. He'll do great things in and through you.

Precious Lord,

I'm learning that one of my soul's greatest needs is to find rest in You. Teach me how to do that, Lord. Help me believe—with my whole heart—that it's possible to cultivate a life that spills joy, possibility, confidence, and renewal. I long for a countenance that reflects a heart at rest and a soul at peace. Help me to arrange my days in a way that create time and space for You to speak to me, heal me, and strengthen me. Forgive me for my tendency to give time away as if I have an endless supply. Help me to wisely steward each moment You've entrusted to me. I know now that each day You give me is a sacred gift from Your hand. Change me from the inside out so that I live and love from my convictions and my connection with You and not from the relentless chaos of my culture. My soul finds rest in You alone. My salvation comes from You. I entrust my whole soul to You, Lord. Lead me in the way that I should go. Amen.

Personal Reflection

1. The last time Matthew Barnett was on my show he made this important statement: Never confuse activity for significance or impact. Consider the things that fill your schedule. Make two columns on a sheet of paper: Activities (non-redemptive) / Significance & Impact. As honestly as you're able, make the distinction between your time-wasters and your time-redeemers.

2. What keeps you from making rest a priority? Is it unbelief? Fear? Ask the Lord for a revelation on what drives you past the rest stops He provides.

3. Do you see rest with God as a gift from God? Do you listen for His cues in this area of your life? Or do you feel the need to grab for yourself so that others don't run over you?

4. Can you envision a life of rhythm, of ebb and flow, one that involves regular rest and replenishment? What has to change for you to get there?

A *Wise Word*

Our soul is like a stream of water, which gives strength, direction, and harmony to every other area of our life. When that stream is as it should be, we are constantly refreshed and exuberant in all we do, because our soul itself is then profusely rooted in the vastness of God and his kingdom.[4]

Group Discussion Starters

1. When you consider your life's pace, do you notice a distinct ebb and flow, or do you tend to go the same pace all the time?
2. What replenishes your soul?
3. When was the last time you enjoyed time in God's presence in a way that adjusted your perspective and impacted your soul?
4. Lately have you noticed any exit ramps—opportunities to step away and rest awhile? Explain.
5. What's your biggest time-waster? How do you feel about eliminating it from your life (or reducing your time allotment to it)?

Faith Declaration

I declare in the mighty name of Jesus that I am an anointed, appointed child of God! I am filled with the Holy Spirit and empowered by His love. I walk in the Lord's presence as I live here on earth. I have eyes to see, ears to hear, and a heart to do His will. I refuse to throw my yes around like it doesn't matter. Life is a gift, and my time is a gift.

God invites me to walk with Him and do the next thing He gives me to do. I am loved, called, and fully equipped to live the powerful life God has assigned to me. I refuse the rat race because God has called me to the sacred race. And I will run with holy passion and conviction. In Jesus' name I pray, Amen!

THE SHACKLED

Yes

✦ 5 ✦

Am I Captive?

Say Yes to Living Free

Fear of man is a dangerous trap, but to trust in God means safety.

Proverbs 29:25 TLB

Here's the problem: you're clinging to true things about yourself that simply aren't *that* true. You're elevating things that are merely true—or half true, or true some days but not others—to the level of the "truest." I know you're doing this because I do it too. We all do. It's the human condition. . . . [But] if you don't know the truest thing about yourself, you don't know yourself. And that matters. What you believe about yourself determines how you live.[1]

David Lomas

Many years ago I sat across the room from a pastor's wife who seemed comfortable in her own skin. She laughed a lot, never seemed to take herself too seriously, and truly didn't seem to care what others thought of her. Not in a hardened, wall-building way—but in a more relaxed way—as though she understood her limitations and was at peace with them.

I marveled at her because I was *anything but* that kind of person. I lived with constant angst over others' critiques and comments and sideways glances. Since I really had no idea what *I* thought about myself, I always felt at the mercy of what others thought of me. Right in the middle of our conversation on a different topic, I blurted out, "How did you get that way?"

Her brows arched a bit and she tilted her head. "What way?"

I continued, "You seem so comfortable with who you are. I can tell you like and accept yourself in a healthy way. And though you're considerate of others, it seems that you don't really need them to like you in order to be okay. How'd you get that way?"

I was an inexperienced young mom at the time, and I longed to know her secret. She set down her coffee cup, placed her hands on her knees, and carefully chose her words. "Susie, I've been hurt enough by others to finally know their limitations and mine. I'm learning to love others and myself the way God loves me. But ultimately my hope is in God. I'm so sorry to tell you that there'll be days ahead when people will devastate you, but that's sometimes what it takes to loosen your hold on their opinions of you. One day you'll be far freer in this area than you are now."

She was right. In the days that followed I experienced some of the most painful friendship betrayal and rejection I ever thought possible. Being on the receiving end of gossip and cruel character critique proves to be a powerful catalyst for breaking free from the bondage of others' opinions.

That painful journey became a most sacred one for me. I fell in love with Jesus on a much deeper level. And my capacity to know His love *for me* increased exponentially. Out of that place, I wrote *The Uncommon Woman,* a book that addresses our identity, the love of God, and our tendency to take the common road of pettiness, gossip, and insecurity when we don't comprehend God's great love for us. God used those experiences to do a sanctifying work in my life.

As I dared to examine my own heart and as I observed people around me, I realized two extremes we go to when it comes to the opinions of others.

Either:

- We hand over our identity on a silver platter and say to anyone and everyone we encounter, "Here, you tell me what I'm worth, because I really don't know."

Or:

- We build a wall so high that nothing gets in and no life flows out. We send a hardened message to anyone who dares come near us: "I don't give a flying rip about what you think about me. I don't need your approval to be okay and I never will."

Both of these extremes reveal a very raw fear of man. When considering their relationships, people who understand the healing God has for them embrace this perspective: I will love you with the love of Christ. I will take risks with you. You may even have the power to hurt me because I am willing to open my heart to you. *But you don't get to decide my worth.* Your opinion will not have the power to diminish me, because Jesus has already established me. I have placed Him on the throne of my heart, and He has settled this issue for me. I will not let go of Him, and He will not let go of me.

How do we know if we're in bondage to others' opinions? Licensed counselor Ed T. Welch suggests we ask ourselves the following questions:[2]

- Have you ever struggled with peer pressure?
- Are you overcommitted? Do you find it hard to say no?
- Do you "need" something from your spouse (in a way that controls you)?
- Is self-esteem a critical concern for you?
- Do you ever feel as though you might be exposed as an imposter?
- Do you frequently second-guess your decisions because of what others might think?
- Do you struggle with feeling empty or meaningless?
- Do you get easily embarrassed?
- Do you ever lie? Especially little white lies?
- Are you jealous of other people?
- Do other people often make you angry or depressed?
- Do you avoid people (in a way that controls you)?

Without any condemnation whatsoever, allow yourself to prayerfully work through this list of questions, not as an indictment, but as information. God wants to set you free. We all have little pockets in our souls where lies go to hide. Certain circumstances bring those lies to the surface. And if—when our flawed nature shows—we decide to medicate or compensate, we short-circuit our spiritual growth. But if we marinate in God's presence and let His love seep into the deepest places of our souls, we'll find our soul's most profound needs met *in Him* and *by Him*. That's when healing comes and transformation begins to show.

Sometimes Freedom Takes Time to Show

Quite a number of years after my revelatory conversation with the pastor's wife, I attended the International Christian Retail Show to do several radio interviews on my latest book. Still a fairly new author, I stood in line with what would be considered A-list guests, each of us ready to do our own interviews. I saw Kirk Cameron, Liz Curtis Higgs, and a few others. I hummed a little tune to myself, *One of these things doesn't belong with the others, can you guess which thing just doesn't belong?* I looked around, surprised that I'd been invited to be on this particular national show.

The radio host noticed the expression on my face. After the interview he pulled me aside and said something I'll never forget. He said, "Susie, I can tell you're wondering why you were invited to be on a national show when you're still a fairly new author. I want to tell you why. I met you a while back when you were just getting started, and I could tell that your love for Jesus trumped all of this.

"It was clear to me that you really didn't need me to like you or even approve of you for you to keep your footing. I've met far too many authors whose eyes reveal their desperate need for approval, fame, and acceptance. You have a grounded-ness about you. And I get the feeling that if God asked you to walk away from it all tomorrow, you would. You're someone I wanted to talk with and hear from."

God had been doing a deep, deep work in my life over the years, and I knew He'd been changing me from the inside out. But this man's statement testified to the fact that what God had been doing on the inside was now becoming visible on the outside. Everyone battles with the fear of man to some degree, but God intends to set us free.

Why We Do the Things We Do

I remember a particularly uncomfortable season in life when God pressed in and addressed my attempts to rescue my sense of self-worth. His nudge in my spirit challenged me to quit striving so that I could more deeply know Him as my God (see Psalm 46:10). In other words, I sensed Him saying to me, *Susie, I know you love to help people, but you'll never realize your full capacity to help others as long as your need for approval drives this train. Let's try something: How about every time you're tempted to lift a finger to prove something about yourself, I dare you not to. Engage your faith in those moments and let My approval be enough for you.*

You know what? This challenge sounded exciting and inviting at first, but it proved to be excruciating for me. I had no idea how often I'd relied on my own efforts to prove myself. At a baby shower, I'd step up to help with the dishes only to realize that my sole purpose was to be the *first* to help, because I had to be *that* good. It took more faith for me to sit on my hands and determine that my worth in Christ was unshakable (whether I helped with the dishes or not) than it did to get up, help with the dishes, and then toss aside my good deed as a nice gesture.

Now, please don't misunderstand me. Of course it's great to do good things for others. But when we rely on our efforts to validate our sense of worth, it's like spitting in the lake and then feeling proud that we've created for ourselves a place to swim. When we rely on our efforts, we fall short every time, and we miss the fullness of what Christ did when He purchased our freedom.

This little lesson in motivation proved to be a life-changing one for me. When our identity remains shackled to others' opinions of us, we're not only held captive, but we bow to the idol of approval. How do we break free from the shackles that hold us captive to others' opinions? One sacred faith-step at a time.

First, pray this prayer with me, if you will:

Precious Lord, I come to You humbly, sincerely, and reverently today. I bow before Your beautiful throne, and I say thank You. Thank You for saving me, forgiving me, cleansing me, and redeeming me. Thank You for access to Your presence and Your promises.

Lord, I open my hands to You this day and I ask Your forgiveness for the countless ways I've tried to affirm my own worth. Forgive me for feebly attempting to do what You've so valiantly already done. I receive—wholeheartedly—the masterful, marvelous gift of Your grace. I reject the lie that I can add one single iota to my worth by performing well. I openhandedly receive anew Your great love for and acceptance of me. From this day forward I want my life to count for You. I want my efforts to be in response to the gift I already possess. May my whole life be a thank offering to You because You have healed me through and through. You're the One who's made me new! I rise up in my blessed, beloved identity, and I wrap myself in Your defining grace today. In Your mighty, powerful, redeeming name, I pray, Amen.

Next, spend some time with the Lord; ask Him to show you whose opinions matter too much to you. He will. He wants you to be free more than you want to be free.

When our boys were growing up, Kevin and I used to tell them, "As Christians, it's good for you to have both Christian and non-Christian friends. But you're not allowed to hang out with anyone you don't have the courage to stand up to. If their opinion matters more to you than your convictions, you're not strong enough to walk with them. So pay attention to how the approval of others impacts you." I've had to take that same advice to heart on plenty of occasions.

So how about you? Whose opinions carry more weight than they should? What lengths do you go to in order to manage their impression of you? Take a moment to ask the Lord to show you how to engage your faith in these relationships. In each of these instances, imagine smashing an idol and putting the Lord in His rightful place in your life once more. His opinion matters most, not our own, not that of others. We see as through a glass dimly; the Lord sees every situation clearly.

We must identify and acknowledge a much wider gap in our perspective between man's opinion and God's opinion.

Ask the Lord for a heightened sensitivity to His Spirit, especially in this area of soul freedom. Ask Him to set you free in the deepest, truest way. Embrace an expectancy that God is very much at work in and around you. In the days ahead you'll notice a heightened awareness of your tendency to overcompensate for the sake of your image. Don't get down on yourself; just humble yourself with holy confidence. Open your hands before almighty God and say, "Once again, Lord, I thank You for loving me, right here, right now. You are mine and I am Yours. Your banner over me is love. There's nothing I can do to add to my worth because I'm already established in You."

If it's not the time or the place to pray that kind of prayer, simply open your hands and declare: "You're more than enough for me and I'm glad."

David Lomas writes:

We want to reprioritize so that we don't get our identity from overworking, but God wants to show us that nothing in life can bring us the pleasure and joy of knowing Him. . . . God's vision always goes beyond ours. We are often pursuing the renewal of our circumstances, but God is pursuing the renewal of our entire identity.[3]

Read the following verse slowly and prayerfully: "Behold, You desire truth in the inward parts, and in the hidden part You will make me to know wisdom" (Psalm 51:6 NKJV). What would it be like to encounter God in such a way that you begin to live out of the truth instead of a lie, and you begin to walk in wisdom and authority where you once walked in brokenness and instability? Picture yourself with a newfound strength, conviction, and courage. Imagine how different your day-to-day choices might be.

What would it be like to experience a renewal of your *entire* identity? That's what He's after in us. And it *is* possible.

The reason Jesus desires truth in our inmost being is because that's where most lies go to hide. We can have lies embedded in our souls that we're not even aware of. Those lies become access points for the devil himself, whose focused intent is to steal, kill, and destroy the life that God has offered us. The enemy leverages the lies we believe to our disadvantage. When a lie embeds in our innermost being, we make choices to compensate for that lie, and we diminish ourselves in the process.

- We strive for approval because we believe that we need it to be okay. *(The lie: God's love isn't enough.)*
- We refuse to take risks because our fear is greater than our faith. *(The lie: God's promises aren't enough.)*
- We medicate ourselves with busyness, food, shopping, etc., instead of slowing down long enough to deal with what drives us to strive. *(The lie: God's presence isn't enough.)*

What's at the root of our fear of man? It's unbelief in the love of God. Read the following verses and let these truths seep deep into your soul and bring healing there:

For God has not given us a spirit of fear, but of power and of love and of a sound mind.

2 Timothy 1:7 NKJV

There is no fear in love. But perfect love drives out fear, because fear has to do with punishment. The one who fears is not made perfect in love.

1 John 4:18

So do not fear, for I am with you; do not be dismayed, for I am your God. I will strengthen you and help you; I will uphold you with my righteous right hand.

Isaiah 41:10

Then you will know the truth, and the truth will set you free.

John 8:32

We know we're captive when we're more worried about man's opinions than we are in awe and wonder over God's unfathomable love. This kind of captivity strangles us to the point that we forget about the power of God's presence in our lives. And the enemy likes it that way. His arrowed questions are intended to shoot unbelief into our souls so he can more easily lie to us about the things that matter most. Unbelief makes us vulnerable. Faith makes us mighty in warfare. Unbelief robs us of joy. Faith brings us peace. Unbelief makes us forget who we are. Faith reminds us that we belong to God.

God's Love Guards and Guides

We walk into the devil's trap every time we choose to doubt God and believe man. If we doubt that God is good, and we believe that man's opinion carries more weight than God says it does, we'll stay captive in our cell even though the lock has been blown off and the door is swinging on its hinges.

Here's one of my favorite verses that keeps me focused on God's love and grounded in His truth: "For Your lovingkindness is before my eyes, and I have walked in Your truth" (Psalm 26:3 NKJV).

Picture God's love as a filter through which every single bit of information must flow before you allow it to enter your soul. For example:

- The odd look from a co-worker
- The fight you had with your husband
- The extra ten pounds you're carrying
- The tiff you had with a close friend
- The bill you forgot to pay
- The commitment you had to drop out of because you said yes too fast

All of these scenarios can stir up insecurity or a sense of inferiority. And the greater the level of unbelief in our souls, the more options we give to the enemy to stir up our fears. Eventually we have to deal with those embedded lies so they will be exposed, evicted, and erased from our belief system.

Back to God's love as a filter: When things happen that stir us up, we need to look above them and remember God's love. His love is ever before us, always with us, and nothing will separate us from that priceless love. When we keep His love as the standard, we become selective about the messages we allow into our souls that are contrary to God's love.

Look again at the list of scenarios above, or better yet, think about the scenarios in your own life that leave you feeling unsettled. Consider them for a moment. Now look above them. Look to the One who holds the world in His hand. Guess what? He calls you *by name.*

Remember God's amazing love and awesome power, and talk to your soul about your circumstances: "These things may be true, but *this* is truer still: His banner over me is love. I am fully and completely established in Him. And nothing will ever change that fact."

The second half of Psalm 26:3 reads this way: ". . . and I have walked in Your truth." Imagine how your life would change if your feet were so grounded in God's Word and in His opinion of you that you walked *continually* in the power of His life-changing grace. God's love establishes us and His truth guides us.

Familiarize yourself with God's Word. Memorize verses that speak to your identity and position in Christ. Write them down and put them places where you'll see them often—your bathroom mirror, the dashboard of your car, a kitchen cabinet. In Christ Jesus, you are a spiritual being housed in a physical body! You are mighty in God! You don't have to put up with the constant plague of insecurity and inferiority. You are someone God loves and intends to use mightily . . . if you'll trust Him.

My friend and former radio co-host Dr. Greg Smalley often says when counseling others, "People aren't the source of truth. They may speak the truth or they may lie to you. They may think they're right about you and still be wrong about you. God is the only Source of truth. If someone says something to you that hurts you or leaves you feeling unsettled, go to the Source of truth and find out what He has to say." Amen!

I believe we all need a significant revelation of God's love to set us free from our captivity. But I also believe we need repeated reminders—of who we are to Him, through Him, and because of Him—to keep us on track. If you've been held captive, don't despair. Just walk free through the already-open prison doors. Jesus already paid for your freedom. Embrace God's love wholeheartedly and let it change you from the inside out.

Let's revisit the prayer we prayed earlier. It's perfect for today:

Precious Lord, I come to You humbly, sincerely, and reverently today. I bow before Your beautiful throne, and I say thank You. Thank You for saving me, forgiving me, cleansing me, and redeeming me. Thank You for access to Your presence and Your promises.

Lord, I open my hands to You this day and I ask Your forgiveness for the countless ways I've tried to affirm my own worth. Forgive me for feebly attempting to do what You've so valiantly already done. I receive—wholeheartedly—the masterful, marvelous gift of Your grace. I reject the lie that I can add one single iota to my worth by performing well. I openhandedly receive anew Your great love for and acceptance of me. From this day forward I want my life to count for You. I want my efforts to be in response to the gift I already possess. May my whole life be a thank offering to You because You have healed me through and through. You're the One who's made me new! I rise up in my blessed, beloved identity, and I wrap myself in Your defining grace today. In Your mighty, powerful, redeeming name, I pray, Amen.

Personal Reflection

1. What painful life experiences still impact your soul today?
2. What scenarios most often stir up insecurity and unhealthy self-awareness in you?
3. In what ways do you strive to manage others' opinions of you?
4. How has God healed you, changed you, and made you stronger than you once were?
5. Can you picture yourself having credibility, wisdom, and strength in an area of your life where you've only known weakness? Why or why not? (Read Psalm 51:6 again.)

A *Wise Word*

Consider the voice of the Savior, who loves drowsy, babbling, ignorant, independent, fearful sinners. What does he have to say to you and me when we create our own gods, write our own glory stories, and babble on about our achievements? He touches us and says, 'Rise, and have no *fear*.' . . . He is the one who saves those whose hearts are so fickle that one day they proclaim him king and the next they call for his blood. . . . He is our king, our husband our redeemer, our salvation. Hosanna! Blessed is he who comes in the name of the Lord to bring beloved sinners to life.[4]

Group Discussion Starters

1. Do you think it's possible to be free from the bondage of others' opinions while maintaining a humble, teachable heart (as opposed to a hardened, walled-off heart)? Or do you think this is something everyone will always deal with in some measure until we see Jesus face-to-face?

2. When you find yourself caring too much about what someone might be thinking of you, what's your default response?

3. Do you have a story to share about a time when you gave too much power to another person? Without using names or details that give away too much information, share the basic scenario and what you learned from it.

4. What passage of Scripture has most helped you stand strong in your true identity in Christ?

5. Describe someone who models a freedom from the bondage of others' opinions. What about this person most stands out to you?

Faith Declaration

I declare in the mighty name of Jesus that I am an anointed, appointed child of God! I am filled with the Holy Spirit and empowered by His love. I walk in the Lord's presence as I live here on earth. I have eyes to see, ears to hear, and a heart to do His will. I refuse to throw my yes around like it doesn't matter. Life is a gift, and my time is a gift. God invites me to walk with Him and do the next thing He gives me to do. I am loved, called, and fully equipped to live the powerful life God has assigned to me. I refuse the rat race because God has called me to the sacred race. And I will run with holy passion and conviction. In Jesus' name I pray, Amen!

✤ 6 ✤

The Power of Peer Pressure
Say Yes to Humility

Humble yourselves, therefore, under God's mighty
hand, that he may lift you up in due time.

1 Peter 5:6

The sin resident in the human heart (the fear of
man) wields awesome power. The praise of others—
that wisp of a breeze that lasts for a moment—can
seem more glorious to us than the praise of God.
(Peer Pressure) is perhaps the most tragic form of
the fear of man. . . . *We are more concerned about
looking stupid* (fear of people) *than we are about
acting sinfully* (fear of the Lord).[1]

Edward T. Welch

My sisters' faces pushed up against the window, prodding and
taunting me to go for it. One sister shouted, "You can do it,

Susie! Just do it!" Another sister piped in, "No she can't! She'll never make it! She's too old!" I glanced at my three sisters, looked down at the makeshift balance beam, firmed up my resolve, and decided to go for it.

Like a gymnast ready to end her beam routine, I stretched my arms up overhead hoping they'd give me power and momentum to fly through the air. Hoping to execute a perfect aerial roundoff dismount, I pushed hard off of my left foot, keeping my eyes on the ground as my legs whipped overhead. I landed short, heard a sickening snap, and collapsed on the ground in pain. Grabbing my throbbing leg, I rolled over onto my side and instantly broke out into a cold sweat. *What had I just done?*

My dad shouted out from around the corner, "Who broke a bone? I heard a snap!" My sisters pulled back from the window and rushed to my side. Only a fool would attempt to dismount a flimsy piece of wood propped up only inches off the ground by two plastic paint pails. *What in the world was I thinking? And at thirty years of age, no less!* Turns out, I didn't break a bone, but I did tear a ligament. And in the weeks that followed, I had a nice purple foot, ankle, and calf to show for it.

Someone once said, "The devil drives. The Shepherd leads." My sisters and I have a fun, bantering relationship, and we love to harass each other whenever we get the chance. They didn't drive me to take a flying leap off of a flimsy piece of wood. My ego provided more than enough drive, thank you very much. But my need for their approval definitely motivated me to go beyond my sensibilities.

Right before I jumped, I felt tangled up with a bunch of emotions that unsettled me. Fear. Uncertainty. Stupidity. I'm on my own here. What a dolt.

Isn't that always the way it goes? The group goads you to jump, but you're the one holding the bag in the end. Or, in my case, a frozen bag of corn to bring down the swelling.

Peer pressure compels us to do things we've either not yet thought all the way through, or things that (due to our fear of man) feel too difficult to say no to. How many life-draining obligations, stupid consequences, sinful acts, or even devastating events could be avoided if we had the presence of mind and the inner conviction to pause, pray, and think through the yes we're about to give away?

We put ourselves at risk when the pressure of the crowd impacts us more than the power of our convictions. But imagine if we could retrain ourselves to consider our birthright (an eternally minded life) over the bowl of soup in front of us (a quick, momentary, and perhaps costly indulgence)?

Think about your life and the multiple times you chose to honor your convictions over the crowd. How many enemy plans have come to nothing because you had the presence of mind to choose the path of wisdom over your whims? Doesn't it spur you on to identify your areas of vulnerability and shore your life up all the more? Consider these examples of people who followed wisdom, not foolishness:

- The worn-out, exhausted husband who decides to go home to his family after a long day of work rather than out for drinks with his prodding, partying co-workers.
- The wife who decides to walk away from the friends who constantly tell her that she can do better than the husband she's currently married to.
- The young mom who opts to change the direction of the conversation rather than add fuel to the gossip fire her friends have started.
- The exhausted Sunday school teacher who realizes she's become snarky and prickly, and decides to step down, step back, and remember why she fell in love with Jesus in the first place.

When the crowd pressures us, we need more than good intentions to keep our footing; we need the wisdom and conviction to live by the inner nudge of the Holy Spirit within us. He will always lead us on the most life-giving path the Lord has for us.

As we get to know Jesus, we more easily recognize His voice. And as we learn to trust His voice even above our own whims and sensibilities, we'll have the courage not to position ourselves outside His will, so when we suddenly find ourselves in what could be a compromising situation, we'll have the sense to stand, run, or simply walk away when wisdom and obedience says we should.

The following two verses serve as great reminders that this walk of faith calls us to keep our ear bent toward heaven and our heart set on following Jesus:

> The Lord directs the steps of the godly. He delights in every detail of their lives.
> Though they stumble, they will never fall, for the Lord holds them by the hand.
>
> Psalm 37:23–24 NLT

> Trust in the Lord with all your heart and lean not on your own understanding; in all your ways submit to him, and he will make your paths straight.
>
> Proverbs 3:5–6

We have a very real enemy who seeks our demise. He will use *any* unsuspecting person to influence our choices in a way that drains the life and potential right out of us. Some may try to woo us into sin because they don't want to sin alone. Others will compel us to settle for far less than God would have for us because they don't have the unction to engage their own faith.

Some will pressure us to help out because no one else seems available. Others will critique us for giving away too much of ourselves even though God may be asking us to sacrifice in a way that others don't understand. Some will try to convince us to quit when we've already felt the nudge to keep going. Others will try to pull on us to stay when God has already told us to go.

As long as our need for approval or our fear of disappointing others is stronger than our God-given sense of calling, we will be more moved by the opportunity of the moment or by the pressure of the crowd than we will by the divine direction of God on our lives.

And what's the result? In extreme cases, we may make choices that cost us what we treasure most: family, freedom, friendships, credibility, character, career, etc. In a not-so-extreme yet still costly sense, we may give away our precious time, energy, and gifts to lesser pursuits and leave ourselves worn out and unavailable for the divine invitation God would have offered us for that particular moment.

When we strive out of our insecurities, and when the current of crowd-approval carries us from one place to the next, we wear ourselves out, make ourselves vulnerable, and miss the best of what God has for us.

The Low Door to Freedom

The crowd pressure is one matter, but what about the internal pressure that builds up inside of us? When you think about it, oftentimes our insecurities, unhealed areas, unbelief, and wrong perspectives are what drive us to make hasty decisions and say yes to un-appointed things, more so than the external pressures of the crowd.

I remember a time when I said yes to participating in a Christmas cookie exchange. I felt obligated because my husband's boss's wife had invited me. How kind of her! The problem is,

I had no idea how to bake cookies that all looked like they belonged on the same plate (not to mention the expectation that the cookies taste great and be packaged festively).

Looking back, it seems unfair that the other women in the group had to take home my pitiful-looking cookies while I got to bring home their beauties. It's like they gave me a piece of beautiful pottery and I gave them a hunk of hardened Play-Doh. I'm not much to sing about in the kitchen. The stress I put myself (and my family) through, just to try to pull off something that was nowhere near my gift set, proved downright ridiculous.

I no longer feel obligated to participate in cookie exchanges—for your sake and mine. What freedom!

When our souls are healed and whole, our choices tend to be more life-giving than soul-draining. On the other hand, when we make an idol out of the opinions of others, we give away our gifts, our time, our divine opportunities, and most important, we give away power to others that belongs to God alone.

How do we break free from the bondage of others' opinions and even from the ungodly pressure we put upon ourselves? Instead of trying to prove our enough-ness to ourselves and to everybody else, we bow low and embrace our not-enough-ness before our mighty God in heaven.

It's okay that we have our limits; God knows all about those limits and has made provisions for us every step of the way. In fact, when we're humble enough to acknowledge our need, God is right there to show Himself strong on our behalf.

So how do we respond to an external pressure that doesn't match up with our internal conviction? We humble ourselves before the Living and Most High God. We pray. We ask God to forgive us for our tendency to wander from the beautiful truth about His love. We ask Him for wisdom and strength, and we entrust ourselves once again *to Him*. We embrace afresh God's great grace and His unrelenting love for us.

We remind ourselves—every moment if we have to—that Jesus paid a dear price to set us free from the bondage of others' opinions so that we can live free to be everything He intended us to be.

When we catch ourselves misusing our time, energy, and gifts to impress man or to rescue our sense of self-worth, it's simply time to pause, bow, and reset our course. We humble ourselves before the throne of God; we ask Him to forgive us for making man's opinion (or even our own opinion) more important to us than His.

And then we worship the Lord. We declare Him as God Most High, far above any other thing. We put Him in His rightful place and we embrace His grace to be a work in progress without the condemnation. What a treasured, priceless gift He has given us! Read *The Message* paraphrase of Ephesians 4:30:

> Don't grieve God. Don't break his heart. His Holy Spirit, moving and breathing in you, is the most intimate part of your life, making you fit for himself. Don't take such a gift for granted.

Once we realize our tendency to build idols out of the opinions of others, we'll be more compelled to evaluate our souls— not in a walking-on-eggshells sort of way, but rather in the light of God's love, without fear or condemnation, and with a sincere passion to follow Jesus wholeheartedly.

As soon as we identify an idol in our lives, we smash it, we pray, and we declare once again that we'll have no other gods before the Lord. We don't want to miss His invitation to live a life guided by His daily direction in our everyday moments.

To walk daily and intimately with the Lord—*that's* the healing path God has for us. He'll use our day-to-day encounters to shape us, heal us, and make us into the people He always intended us to be.

When we regularly deal with our tendency to elevate man's opinion over God's opinion, our spiritual eyes will open and we'll more easily discern God's best path for our lives. Fear stirs up our insecurities and drives us to strive. Love opens our eyes and invites us to respond.

We're really not even capable of loving others the way Christ loves them until His opinion matters most to us. Read Ed T. Welch's insight on this point:

> Regarding other people, our problem is that we *need* them (for ourselves) more than we *love* them (for the glory of God). The task God sets before us is to need them *less* and love them *more*. Instead of looking for ways to manipulate others, we will ask God what our duty is toward them.[2]

Our goal is to find such freedom and wholeness in Christ alone that we truly enjoy the way He loves us, which freely enables us to spill out His love to others. Paul writes in Ephesians that to know this love *is to be filled* with the fullness of God. Read this powerful passage:

> And may you have the power to understand as all God's people should, how wide, how long, how high, and how deep his love is. May you experience the love of Christ, though it is too great to understand fully. Then you will be made complete with all the fullness of life and power that comes from God.
>
> Ephesians 3:18–19 NLT

When we're filled with the fullness of God, we spill His love as an almost involuntary response. Have you met people who love like that? The passion and love of Jesus oozes out of their pores without their even trying to be or appear a certain way. I want to be around those kinds of people because they remind me of how God feels about me. And I want to be someone who does that same thing for everyone I meet.

We love because He loved us first. And to the extent that we wrap our hearts and minds around so great a love as this, will we begin to love others the way Christ loves them.

Since our worth and identity are settled issues, we don't have to get tangled up in the constant drama of high offendability and posturing insecurity common to so many people. We break free from the bondage of others' opinions so we can turn around and love them in spite of themselves. Want an added bonus? We no longer need them to validate who we are.

The Way Up Is Down

Think about it for a moment. Why do we care so much what others might think of us? And why do we alternate from thinking too highly of ourselves to thinking so terribly about ourselves, sometimes in only a matter of minutes? Why do the ever-changing opinions of other flawed human beings seem to have the power to hold us captive and steal our joy?

I think it's because we forget that we are heirs. When we forget who we are—children of the living God, sons and daughters of the Most High God—we find ourselves constantly carried along by the waves of performance and approval, which change every time the winds blow.

We don't want to be considered "less than," so we attempt to prove that we are more than others think we are, more than we actually believe ourselves to be. The problem is, most of the time we're wrong—about others and about ourselves. We're all more sinful than we could possibly understand and more loved than we could ever comprehend. So when we feel less-than and we attempt to prove others wrong and prove ourselves wrong, we become like a dog chasing his tail. Our need to prove ourselves takes us in a circle until we've chased ourselves silly.

When others seem to slight us or overlook us or pressure us to do their agenda ahead of what God has asked us to do, the answer isn't to get big, it's to get small.

The only safe place for a vulnerable soul is at the feet of Jesus. If you feel overlooked or pushed around by others' strong opinions, and it stirs up something in you, it's because that "something" in you needs a reminder of your birthright. This is when you grab a fistful of your shirt right over your heart and say loud enough for your ears to hear, "Christ *in me* is my hope of glory! My adoption into the family of God is *not* up for grabs. I will live like the heir I am." A bowl of soup (your immediate desire met) will not strengthen you like the truth about your adoption will.

I've finally learned how powerful and sacred it is to glory in my low position. Let me explain. When others overlook me, don't include me, or forget about me for some reason, I may feel invalidated. My fleshly instinct is to stand up on a chair so I look taller than I am in an attempt to validate myself. But that gets me nowhere and makes me look like an adolescent.

Now I finally understand that these are perfect times to be acquainted with my Savior. One day I was feeling sore over the rude treatment from another author/speaker, and the Lord whispered these words to my heart: *My child, now's the perfect time to glory in your low position. I'm with you in this place. I dwell in and with the humble, broken heart. I'm nearest to those the world overlooks. Be much with Me here. You don't need her approval to be mighty in God. Besides, I absolutely love the story I'm writing with your life. I'm the One who will establish you. Be much with Me here. Trust Me here.*

And let me tell you, I found beautiful, bursting life in that low, invisible place. When the world overlooks me, I know that God sees me. Really embrace this important truth: To know God's intimate and profound love on a deeper level is not the consolation prize for being overlooked. It's the actual treasure we'd hoped to find when we sought the approval and admiration of others in the first place.

> For a day in Your courts is better than a thousand.
> I would rather be a doorkeeper in the house of my God
> Than dwell in the tents of wickedness.
>
> Psalm 84:10 NKJV

When others overlook you, be wise enough to glory in that low position. Find Jesus there with you. He can teach you something profound in that place. And when the time is right, He'll lift you up and bless you before a watching world.

> Humble yourselves, therefore, under God's mighty hand, that he may lift you up in due time.
>
> 1 Peter 5:6

Want to ensure your captivity? Set your thoughts on the actual or potential disapproval of others. It'll put fear in your heart and angst in your soul. You'll begin to make captive-minded choices because you'll perceive your value and worth from a captive's point of view.

Want to ruin your life? Let the crowds and the committees pressure you into helping out every time there's a need. Give away all of your time until you run yourself so ragged that you lose your joy and faith perspective, and the outside world questions if Jesus has really made a difference in your life.

Want to walk free? Set your mind on things above. Set your heart on the unchanging, indisputable truth of God's love for you. Do the next thing He tells you to do. If He says rest, then rest. If He says run, then run. With all your might. If He says wait, then surrender control, open your hands, and entrust Him with the timing of your breakthrough. Worship Him in the meantime. Walk in the fear of the Lord and you will walk free.

We've got to dare to ask ourselves: What's more important, our status before men or our status before God? We've got to wrestle this one to the ground and hold fast to a right perspective lest it get away from us. Something beautiful happens when we shift all of our value onto the One who made us.

When we wrap our hearts around God's love for us and His intentions for us, He can use us to do great things without it going to our head. We can lead with courage, humility, and conviction. And when we are slighted, overlooked, or displaced, we can endure it without falling into the ditch of despair.

There'll be chapters in our stories where others wrongly assess us. But God *always* deeply loves and understands us. And that needs to be enough for us. Can we be content to be misunderstood if we know we're in the center of God's will? Those are the times and places where heroes are born.

Jesus refused to put any weight whatsoever on the opinions of man. He cared deeply for their souls but did not—for a moment—need their approval.

> I do not accept glory from human beings. . . . How can you believe since you accept glory from one another but do not seek the glory that comes from the only God?
>
> John 5:41, 44

In his brilliant book *Humility*, Andrew Murray wrote this:

> Nothing can cure you of the desire to receive glory from men or of the sensitivities and pain and anger that come when it's not given, but seeking alone the glory that comes from God. Let the glory of the all-glorious God be everything to you. You will be freed from the glory of men and of self and be content and glad to be nothing. Out of this nothingness you will grow strong in faith, giving glory to God, and you will find that the deeper you sink in humility before Him, the nearer He is to fulfill every desire of your faith.[3]

Jesus invites you to a life of intimacy with Him. As you walk closely with Him, you'll learn—on an ever-increasing level— who He is and who you are because of Him. The more deeply you get to know Him, the more profoundly you'll consider your yes as sacred and set apart.

Precious Lord,
You are all I need. You are more than enough for me! I worship You this day! I lift You up and put You in Your proper place—high above the opinions of man, high above my opinions of myself—and I declare once again that You, O God, are the Lord of my life. Forgive me for my feeble attempts to manage my image and my identity. Forgive me for giving away time in an effort to manage others' opinions of me. You gave me gifts and time to steward for Your kingdom purposes. I ask You, Lord, heal me in the deepest places of my soul. Give me a fresh revelation of Your great love for me. Help me to know it from the top of my head to the tips of my toes. May I be so acquainted with how You feel about me that it puts joy in my heart and a spring in my step. May holy confidence and humble dependence mark my life in every way. Father, do such a deep work in me that when others encounter me, they encounter You. Thank You for loving me like You do. Help me to live like the heir I am. In Jesus' name, I pray, Amen.

Personal Reflection

1. When you think about how peer pressure impacted you (either positively or negatively), what memory most stands out in your mind? What did you learn about yourself from that experience?

2. In what area of life do you feel most susceptible to peer pressure (friends, church leaders, your kids' coaches, co-workers, etc.)?

3. In what ways have you compromised your convictions in these relationships (in ways big or small)?

4. Can you identify ways that you've let your guard down in these relationships (with regard to who you are in Christ and what He's called you to)?

5. God wants to strengthen you in the deepest places of your soul so you can show up in these relationships with a new level of holy confidence and humble dependence. What do you sense He's saying to you about your perspective on these relationships?

A *Wise Word*

We can be religious and do all sorts of things for God, but if these are not done in humble dependence on Christ, they will amount to nothing. We need to relinquish our control over 'what we do for God,' and trust wholly in what God does in and through us as we live and walk by faith. Finally, our worth is also found in relinquishing control of our spiritual image or reputation. Our worth comes in joining the rest of the human race—in coming down off our spiritual pedestals and giving up the constant attempt to establish our value in comparison to other people.[4]

Group Discussion Starters

1. Share about a time from your childhood when you gave in to peer pressure and wish you hadn't. How did it turn out?

2. Share about a time when you stood up for your convictions amidst the pressure of a person or the crowd.

3. Talk about a time when you said yes to too many things and you ended up overwhelmed. What compelled you to say yes?

4. How did the overload impact you and your family? Do you approach your commitments differently now? Why or why not?

5. In what areas of life do you want to shore up your resolve to say no to un-appointed obligations (things God never asked you to do) so you can say yes to the divine invitations God has for you?

Faith Declaration

I declare in the mighty name of Jesus that I am an anointed, appointed child of God! I am filled with the Holy Spirit and empowered by His love. I walk in the Lord's presence as I live here on earth. I have eyes to see, ears to hear, and a heart to do His will. I refuse to throw my yes around like it doesn't matter. Life is a gift, and my time is a gift. God invites me to walk with Him and do the next thing He gives me to do. I am loved, called, and fully equipped to live the powerful life God has assigned to me. I refuse the rat race because God has called me to the sacred race. And I will run with holy passion and conviction. In Jesus' name I pray, Amen!

7

Do You See What He Sees?

Say Yes to Your Worth

For we are God's masterpiece. He has created us
anew in Christ Jesus, so we can do the good things
he planned for us long ago.

Ephesians 2:10 NLT

The reality is that God does not send slaves to the
Promised Land. That place is reserved for daughters
and sons. We can know Promised Land living only
after we get our identity straight. He has abundance
and richness and life that is *truly* life in store for us.
If only we will learn to live free.[1]

Brady Boyd

Rumor has it that Vincent van Gogh occupies a branch in
our family tree. He didn't have any children, so the potential
relationship would come through his siblings. I've never done

the research necessary to find out if I'm truly related to this amazing yet troubled artist, but the very idea of it intrigued my son enough to study van Gogh's life and come to appreciate his work. Van Gogh's masterpiece *Starry Night* has absolutely captured Jake's heart. He says that every time he looks at this scene, he either gets a lump in his throat or his eyes well up with tears. If you've never seen this painting, you'll have to Google it. In fact, take a moment right now to look at *Starry Night* so you can better understand the point I'm about to make. When I asked Jake what about the painting moves him so, he shared,

> *Starry Night* reminds me of two things: first, that our world is so small and surrounded by chaos as shown by the active sky in the painting, but we can't put it in a box or categorize it so we shouldn't try; and second, that God is in the chaos and can't be categorized or controlled either. To quote van Gogh, "Paintings have a life of their own that derives from the painter's soul."
>
> God's creation is a masterful reflection of who He is as the Creator. It reminds me how small but loved and protected we are. We live our sometimes-small lives on this relatively small planet, and God loves us deeply amidst our everyday moments. And we're not left to ourselves here. Spiritual activity swirls around us, and so often we're not even aware of it. God is in everything, from the flickering candlelight in a small French village to every corner of the infinite cosmos. *Starry Night* serves as a reminder to pay attention.

Well said, son! Don't we all need reminders to pay attention? What happens when we get too busy and run too hard tending to tasks God never asked us to do?

We wear ourselves out with little fruit to show for all of our striving. We lose our God-given sense of awe and wonder. We stop paying attention to God's very real involvement in our story. We no longer notice God's handiwork. We quit looking for Him with expectancy. We miss out on the sacred moments He provides. And we forget that miracles exist all around us.

Do you remember the last time you slowed down long enough to take in the intricate details of a butterfly's wing? Or the last time you stopped in your tracks and pondered the miracle of childbirth? Our world experiences that particular miracle three to four times *every second* of every day.

Have you paused lately to consider that when you worship—I mean, really worship from the depths of your heart and with all the passion in your soul—that your heartfelt cry actually ignites movement in the heavenly realm? And that God draws near because He loves it when you sing to Him?

Elizabeth Barrett Browning wrote these insightful words: "Earth's crammed with heaven, and every common bush afire with God, but only he who *sees* takes off his shoes. The rest sit round and pluck blackberries."[2]

Not only that, *you* count as one of God's miracles walking the earth today. You are His masterpiece, created brand-new in Christ Jesus, first and foremost because He loves to create beautiful works of art, and second, because He loves to communicate the miracle of His love through a masterpiece like you.

A Closer Look

Picture yourself standing at the Museum of Modern Art in New York City. You're standing in front of van Gogh's *Starry Night*, taking in the intricacies of this painting. You take a closer look at the small town and imagine its people turning in for the night, weary from a long day's work, unsuspecting of the spiritual activity that swirls around them. You ponder the whole idea of God's very real presence in your life. You embrace the idea that He initiates spiritual activity in the heavenly realms *on your behalf.*

For the first time in a long time, you get a glimpse of how deeply you're known, loved, and tended to by our living, loving Creator-God. You breathe in the wonder of it all. *Oh, to know this love is to be filled with the fullness of God.*

While you revel in your thoughts, a man and woman briskly walk behind you on their way to look at another painting in the museum. You notice how much more put-together and at ease they seem than you picture yourself to be. You look back at the painting and imagine yourself in that little town, living your life from your earthbound perspective.

You zero in on one of the little houses in the painting, then picture the inside of your house and all the projects that are still on your list of to-do's: the pile of laundry billowing over, begging for your attention; the refrigerator light that needs to be replaced; the extra pounds you keep promising yourself you'll lose, starting tomorrow . . . and you breathe a heavy sigh.

Suddenly you hear a ruckus behind you, and you turn around to see a couple of teens standing on the other side of the museum, pointing your way and making fun of the masterpiece in front of you. With a loud voice they spout, "What's so great about that painting? It looks like a bunch of swirls and splotches. Like a finger-painting project. Any kindergartener could do better." You look back at the painting and you realize something. The adolescents are right about the swirls and splotches. Those are there. But they're completely wrong in their assessment. Whether they know it or not, *Starry Night* is a masterpiece. A work of art. And suddenly you realize, so are you.

Picture van Gogh next to you with his hand on your shoulder. He leans in and shows you all of the detail and nuance of this particular masterpiece. The more you learn about his intent, the more you appreciate the brilliance of his work. As you listen to him excitedly tell you about the quaintness of the town and activity in the sky, you suddenly care very little what the teen boys have to say.

Stick with me for another moment in this analogy. Notice the two perspectives that can derail us:

- When we assess ourselves from the inside, from too close a perspective—apart from God's love for us—and thus despair over the flaws we see and feel
- When we let others assess us from a distance, and we take to heart their opinions because they've observed a few surface things about us that we've noticed too

When you look at your life from the inside of your mess—and apart from God's involvement in your life—your assessment will always be incomplete. And when others toss out their assessments of you based on partial information, their assessments will always be incorrect.

Don't let the reality of your beauty fall underfoot like a used gum wrapper simply because you don't feel or see your worth quite yet. Trust me. Better yet, trust God when He says that you're worth far more than you can even comprehend. And don't give away your power to those who know you either from a distance or through a skewed lens. They only know in part.

Imagine Jesus up close and personal, with His arm around you, taking you through your story. He's intimately familiar with and involved in every detail of your life.

You can be partially right about a painting and still be completely wrong about its value, when you see only a portion of what the artist intended. It's like taking a sentence out of context and judging it apart from the message and the messenger. People who stand at a distance and pride themselves on their acute ability to assess and constantly critique others are like static in God's ears. And the truth is, most of the time they don't know what they're talking about.

Sometimes we (or others) assess our value outside the context of God's loving intent for our lives. And though we (or others) may be right about a few things, we'll be wrong about the main thing, the one thing we must not forget: We are made by Creator-God for His divine purposes. No matter what anyone else thinks about us. We are image bearers of the Most High God.

These things are true about you, even when they don't feel true:

- *You* are a masterpiece, created by God Himself, for a very distinct purpose.
- The heavenly realm is close. God is nearer than you think—even when you least grasp or suspect it.
- Spiritual activity is happening all around you, for you, and because of you.
- Jesus cares deeply for you. He's mighty and powerful and intimately near you.

When we compare our insides to everyone else's outsides, we will always come up short. The truth is, *anybody's* internal process will look vastly different and far messier than someone else's external presentation. Thanks to makeup, cute clothes, and a great pair of shoes, women can cover up a whole lot of what's going on inside. Men have their own varieties of camouflage. Some of us work harder than others to look better on the outside than we often feel on the inside. Either way, how we look and how we feel are two very different things.

Yet as Christ-followers, we have no business relying on our external abilities to validate our internal worth. Nor should we consider our feelings and internal journey as indicators of who we are or how valuable we are unless we do so with an awe and wonder of how far we've come because of Christ in us.

Though the weight of our humanness compels us to look down and focus on the tangibles in front of us, Jesus invites us to look up and lay claim to the promises He's offered us.

We must not judge ourselves based on partial information. Nor should we assess our worth or determine our identity while looking at all of the unfinished business in our lives. I've said this before; can I say it again? We are works in progress. And we get to be. Without the condemnation.

All of our emotions, memories, and regrets, and all of our passions, hopes, and dreams—they're all tangled up together because we're works in progress. And Jesus is deeply, profoundly invested in helping us sort through our story so that we can live free. He knows we're works in progress, yet He lovingly, patiently sticks with us every step of the way. And He's not going anywhere.

He'll see your story all the way through to its beautiful conclusion.

Just the other day I stumbled upon this passage, and it made me gasp.

> But our High Priest offered himself to God as a single sacrifice for sins, good for all time. Then he sat down in the place of honor at God's right hand. There he waits until his enemies are humbled and made a footstool under his feet. For by that one offering he forever made perfect those who are being made holy.
>
> Hebrews 10:12–14 NLT

Jesus' victory over our sin and our death is good for *all time*. And by that one offering, He has made us forever perfect, while we're being made holy. He's made us perfect while we're being-made-holy. He's made you perfect, while you're: *Being. Made. Holy.* Let that sink in.

You're a child of the Most High God. You're an heir of God. A joint heir with Christ. You're perfect in His sight, in right standing before a Most Holy God. And you're in process, being made holy as you put your hope in Him and trust Him to make you new. "All who have this hope in him purify themselves, just as he is pure" (1 John 3:3).

In her excellent book *A Million Little Ways*, Emily Freeman writes:

> We want to live a beautiful life that means something. We want to create and love and move on purpose. We want to make art. We know we are image bearers and our hands itch for the job we were made to do. But we cannot push results ahead of receiving. We cannot dig in our heels against the natural rhythm of the sea and expect to win, stretch out stiff arms in the face of God and refuse to receive what He has to offer. . . . We are made in the image of God and are being remade inside the person of Jesus Christ. He holds all things together even when it looks like they're falling apart. His grace fills in my lack.[3]

Eyes Up

When you live tethered to an earthbound mindset, it only takes a moment to lose perspective and get discouraged. When your laser focus zeroes in on your unpaid bills, the number on your scale, your inattentive spouse, your unfulfilled desire, or your wayward kids—before you know what happened or why—your whole day goes south and you forget who you are.

We all have parts of our lives that we wish were different. We all carry around in our hearts a measure of grief from regrets, hurts, heartbreaks, and disappointments. We feel the ache in our soul when things don't go the way we'd hoped. We feel frustrated with ourselves when we stumble in the same ways we have for years. What's the answer? Look up. Ask Jesus to help us see the worth in our story, the worth in our souls, because we belong to Him.

Oftentimes at my speaking events I have women and men put their hand over their hearts and repeat after me:

- I'm not who I was.
- I'm not what I do.
- I'm someone He enjoys.

And then we say it again. It seems the words sink in a little better the second time around. Here's the truth about you:

You're not a sum of your past mistakes. You're not the accumulation of your grand achievements. You're not your family tree. You're not your flaws. You're not even your virtues. You're a masterpiece made by God Himself. You're someone He loves. You're someone He cared enough about to create, redeem, and establish for the earth today. You're prized, loved, accepted, called, equipped, and sent. You're blessed to be a blessing.

Need biblical proof that you have otherworldly value no matter what you feel about yourself or what others think they know about you? Here's some:

- You are alive in Christ and forgiven of your sins (Colossians 2:13). Say it: *I am alive in Christ Jesus, totally and completely forgiven of my sins! I will not let my past speak to me except to teach me! I am fully alive in Christ!*
- You are NOT condemned for your past mistakes and sins. The law of the Spirit of God has set you free from the law of sin and death (Romans 8:1–2). Say it: *I refuse any condemnation the enemy throws my way! I am free from the law of sin and death! I am loved, forgiven, and free!*
- You are blessed with every spiritual blessing in the heavenly realms (Ephesians 1:3). Say it: *I am blessed beyond measure, rich beyond comprehension! I will live the full life God has promised me!*

- You have access to the throne room of God, and you can approach Him with freedom and confidence (Hebrews 4:16). Say it: *I have access to the inner throne room of Almighty God! I can approach Him with freedom and confidence and be assured of His glad welcome. He loves me, is there for me, and will never forsake me!*
- You have the Spirit of the Living God within you to help you discern who you are and what you possess in Christ Jesus (1 Corinthians 2:12). Say it: *I am full of the power of the Holy Spirit within me! He opens my eyes—more and more every day—so I can understand and grasp all that belongs to me because I belong to Jesus! I grow daily in the knowledge of God because His Spirit lives in me!*
- You're equipped to do more than just get by. You're equipped to be more than a conqueror. Why? Because He loves you! (Romans 8:37) Say it: *I am more than a conqueror in Jesus Christ! Though I face many trials, I will overcome every one of them because I am mighty in God and He is mighty in me!*
- You are loved and empowered beyond comprehension (Ephesians 3:16–19). Say it: *I am filled to the fullness of God! I am loved deeply and profoundly! And I will live like the heir I am!*
- You are invited to dream with God and give Him access to your story (Ephesians 3:20–21). Say it: *I invite You, Lord, to do a miracle in and through me! Do above and beyond all I could ever dare to ask or think! I will—by faith—live a life totally disproportionate to who I am because Christ Jesus lives in me!*

We could do this all day (and in truth, some days we need to), but I think you get the point. You are a treasured vessel created

by the one and only masterful, star-breathing God. He has set
His affections upon you. He intends to use you to do great
things. But not in the sense of using you up and running you
ragged. He wants to fill you up, pour you out, and transform
you as you go. Jesus Himself said so. "Whoever believes in
me, as Scripture has said, rivers of living water will flow from
within them" (John 7:38).

Read this masterful paraphrase of Hebrews 6:13–18 by Eugene Peterson:

> When God made his promise to Abraham, he backed it to the
> hilt, putting his own reputation on the line. He said, "I promise
> that I'll bless you with everything I have—bless and bless and
> bless!" Abraham stuck it out and got everything that had been
> promised to him. When people make promises, they guarantee
> them by appeal to some authority above them so that if there
> is any question that they'll make good on the promise, the au-
> thority will back them up. When God wanted to guarantee
> his promises, he gave his word, a rock-solid guarantee—God
> can't break his word. And because his word cannot change, the
> promise is likewise unchangeable.
>
> We who have run for our very lives to God have every reason
> to grab the promised hope with both hands and never let go.[4]

Here's the NIV version of Hebrews 6:19: "We have this hope
as an anchor for the soul, firm and secure. It enters the inner
sanctuary behind the curtain." Think about that for a moment.
You are anchored to God in *heaven.* Your soul is anchored upward to your final destination and the anchor holds. Dr. Wiersbe
writes: "We are anchored upward—to heaven—not downward.
We are anchored, not to stand still, but to move ahead! Our
anchor is 'sure'—it cannot break—and 'steadfast'—it cannot
slip. No earthly anchor can give that kind of security!"[5]

Picture yourself anchored upward and forward. He holds you
secure because He values you so deeply. Do you see what God

sees when He looks at you? If not, don't despair; just press in and ask God for a fresh revelation of His love and fresh insight into your divine worth in Him.

From time to time, we all forget what we look like to Him. Sometimes He pours out fresh grace and we can actually feel the truth of our worth. But other times He asks us to walk by faith in the absence of any feeling whatsoever. Those are tough times—when all of the messages coming our way seem to contradict what we know to be true.

Can you hold on to the promise even then? He's got you even if you forget. Or let go. But when you hold on, your faith gets stronger and your resolve firmer. If you hold on to God's perspective—especially when it doesn't feel true—your ability to live by the reality of your divine worth will grow steadily.

Can we do this for each other? Instead of our perpetual tendency to compare ourselves to each other, to isolate when we feel insecure, and to diminish our lives by our own wrong perspectives, let's sing God's song to each other. Let's remind each other that we—as in process as we are—are made in *His image*. We're on a pilgrimage to a most holy destination. And in the meantime, let's help each other see the true worth we each possess.

Notice God's artistry all around you. Ask God to help you see His unique handiwork in you and others. Look for it in the eyes of a stranger, and be kind. Embrace and love friends when they seem distant and unavailable. Maybe they're hurting and need your love more than your frustration. Give others the benefit of the doubt, and give yourself a bit more grace too. We're on our way home.

At the beginning of the chapter I quoted my friend, pastor Brady Boyd. Now that you've given more thought to your precious worth in Christ, let's read Brady's words one more time and take them in a little deeper this time:

The reality is that God does not send slaves to the Promised Land. That place is reserved for daughters and sons. We can know Promised Land living only after we get our identity straight. He has abundance and richness and life that is *truly* life in store for us. If only we will learn to live free.[6]

We are anchored upward and forward. May we live as ones who are spoken for. Treasured. Tried. And True.

Precious Lord,
Help me to grasp the awesome truth about who I am!
Awaken my heart to the artistry You intended when You
made me. Forgive me for the countless times I've altogether
missed what You've entrusted to me. You've given me life,
the treasure of today, and gifts to share with a world in
need. I'm so sorry that I've allowed unbelief and insecu-
rity to drive me to say yes for all the wrong reasons. I will
no longer live to please others or squander my precious
time to manage others' opinions of me. You paid a huge
price for my freedom, which means I'm no longer a slave
to the opinions of others. Help me to live, breathe, and
embrace life like the child of God I am. I'm anchored to
You, and You to me. Upward and forward I go because
You love me. Thank You, Lord. Amen.

Personal Reflection

1. Would you say that most of your thoughts about yourself are kind and hopeful? Or are they critical and demeaning? What do you attribute that to?
2. What do you suppose God loves most about the way He created you?
3. When do you most easily lose confidence or sight of your divine value (comparison, failure, fatigue, etc.)?

4. Can you think of a time when you felt most aware of God's pleasure over you and love for you? Why do you suppose that was?

5. Jesus calls us to love Him and love others as we love ourselves. What does it mean to love ourselves? How well do you love yourself?

A Wise Word

When we understand that we were created for His divine purpose, our eyes become more focused on what matters. We become enveloped in His relentless love for us, and we get passionate about where He is taking us. We expect to encounter a few bumps along the way, but we finally believe that bumps, bruises, and deep valleys are not defining factors for us. Yes, they mark our journey and shape us into kingdom people, but they do not have the power to diminish our value.[7]

Group Discussion Starters

1. When was the last time you stopped in awe over some of God's handiwork (e.g., the sky, a sunset, a flower, your child)? Explain.

2. This question might be a bit uncomfortable for you, but I dare you to try to answer it: How would the world be different if you weren't here? Place yourself in the lead role of *It's a Wonderful Life* and imagine what life would have been like for others without you. Why is the world a blessed place because you exist? In what ways has God used you to communicate His love? Take time to think this through.

3. Describe someone you know and greatly admire. How do you see God's handiwork in his or her life?

4. Consider those who know you and really love you. How would they describe God's handiwork in your life? Are you quick to dismiss and qualify their comments, or are you able to embrace them with your whole heart?

5. How can you more deeply engage your faith as it relates to your divine worth and calling? What scriptural truth do you most need to hang on to? (Refer to the list of verses and declarations earlier in the chapter.)

Faith Declaration

I declare in the mighty name of Jesus that I am an anointed, appointed child of God! I am filled with the Holy Spirit and empowered by His love. I walk in the Lord's presence as I live here on earth. I have eyes to see, ears to hear, and a heart to do His will. I refuse to throw my yes around like it doesn't matter. Life is a gift, and my time is a gift. God invites me to walk with Him and do the next thing He gives me to do. I am loved, called, and fully equipped to live the powerful life God has assigned to me. I refuse the rat race because God has called me to the sacred race. And I will run with holy passion and conviction. In Jesus' name I pray, Amen!

✧ 8 ✧

There's Freedom in God's Yes

Say Yes to God's Best

For the Lord is the Spirit, and where the Spirit of
the Lord is, there is freedom.

2 Corinthians 3:17 NLT

Every action we take in life has a sense of identity
behind it. How we see ourselves matters.[1]

David Lomas

My dreams ended up on hold for the moment. At first they
seemed within my reach, right at my fingertips. Then my pastor
and his wife asked us out to breakfast. My husband and I love
this couple and cherish any time we have with them. We savored
our eggs and hashbrowns and enjoyed lighthearted conversation. Then came the invitation: *We've been praying about it,
and we're wondering if you'd consider taking over the youth
ministry for us. We think you'd do a great job with our kids. I*

sat back in the booth and thought for a moment. I longed to write a book someday. An agent had recently contacted me and expressed interest in working with me. It seemed my toes had finally touched the edges of my promised land.

Yet there I sat, across the table from two people whom I deeply respect. How could I tell them no? But I had to. The desires of my heart beckoned, and God had opened a door I'd waited a long time to walk through.

I leaned in and opened my mouth to speak, when suddenly I strongly sensed the Lord's direction in my spirit: *Wait. Do not say no. Tell them you'll pray about it.*

But I didn't want to pray about it! I love teens, yes. But I'd been praying for many seasons about my call and my purpose. The more I prayed, the stronger the desire to hunker down and write grew within me. Plus, the chance to work with a literary agent was finally right in front of me! Still, I knew what I had to do. So I asked for some time to pray about their invitation. And I did.

You can imagine my surprise when God nudged me to set aside my dream for a time so I could step up and help with the youth. I wrestled with the dichotomy: God placed in my heart a strong desire to communicate His truths through writing, but then He asked me to lay it aside and take on a significant time commitment—one that challenged my will and *seemed* to interrupt and postpone His own plans for me. But I'd spent enough time with Him to know His voice—and to trust what He commanded. The truth was, I really didn't want anything He didn't want for me. And I didn't want my own selfish tendencies to get in the way of an opportunity to partner with Him in a way that could change lives.

I tell the rest of this story in a couple of my other books. You can read about my ego-bruising adventure another day. But suffice to say, God used that season of service to refine me in ways that were painful, beautiful, humbling, and critical to the future call on my life.

I longed for my own dreams to come true, and suddenly the opportunity appeared before my very eyes. Even so, God had a different plan. He intended for my husband and me to sow into the lives of teens—many of whom had dreams of their own. We saw God do a beautiful work in the lives of our youth. We felt honored and privileged to have a place in their hearts. During those years of dying to myself so that life could spring forth in others, I learned a valuable kingdom lesson. As Christ followers, we are not too small for big things, and not too big for small things.

But then one day, several years later, the winds of change started to blow. I sensed God's whisper in my heart to pick up where I left off and start the writing process again. I adjusted my time commitments and made room in my day to put words on the page. But this time, I wrote from a different place in my soul. I understood—on a deeper level—that my times were in God's hands.

I learned that because my life belongs to Him, He gets to decide where my time, gifts, and talents are spent.

We serve a mighty and awesome God. If we're serious about following His direction in our lives, then He gets to say—from day to day—how we live, how we give, how we serve, how we pray, what we say, and what we do with our day. Jesus is the hope of the earth. His dreams and His purposes matter most whether we understand them or not.

Invitation or Obligation?

I had a lot to learn about the craft of writing. We scraped together enough money to send me to a writer's conference. I learned how to write a book proposal. I enjoyed the discipline of putting words on the page and the grind of tightening up my message. I still served at church but in a more limited capacity. One day a church leader approached me and asked me why I wasn't serving at a more involved level. Keep in mind, I taught aerobics part time, had three active school-aged sons, and a house to keep clean, plus I already served on two committees at church. I couldn't manage another obligation and keep my commitment to writing, which, I strongly sensed, was God's invitation to me. I'd waited on His timing, and He'd finally given me the go-ahead. His grace abounded in me amidst the writing process.

As I explored the unknown territory of writing, God revealed His heart to me in such a precious, intimate way that over time, even more important than my desire to get published was my desire to be in the center of His will in every aspect of my life. Waiting and watching for the Lord, and then following His lead, became the most important and significant things I could do with my moments and my days. And I learned something about His provision and His character every sacred step of the way.

After I explained to this church leader why I couldn't take on another commitment, he asked about the time I spent working on this writing dream of mine. He asked if I had a publisher yet.

I answered, "Well, no. Not at the moment. I'm still working on my proposal." He surprised me with his next question.

With a hand on his hip and a smug look on his face, he asked, "You mean to tell me, you'd waste the Lord's valuable time on a dream to get published *someday*? Are you telling me you're willing to throw away your time over the next few months in hopes that this 'dream' *might* come true?"

Honestly, his perspective shocked me. But I'd been so refined during the waiting process that I knew God had me right in the center of His will. I replied, "I'd not only 'waste' months on this dream, I'd waste years on it, if that's what God asked of me. I know writing is a part of His plan for me. It's not my own self-ambitious goal."

He looked thoroughly disgusted and irritated with me, but that only bothered me a little. I stayed the course, listened to the Lord, took my steps as He directed me, and eventually got published. The letters and emails I receive from readers are the fruit from that hidden season of trusting God and giving Him my yes—both when it suited me and when it didn't.

When my pastor and his wife asked us to oversee the youth ministry, they issued an invitation. And I knew they'd continue to love us no matter if we said yes or no. But I also knew they'd prayed about it. Since this couple walks so intimately with the Lord, they heard Him when He pointed us out to help with the youth. Though teaching young people wasn't what I initially wanted to do during that particular season of life, it was God's invitation to me. To both my husband and me.

We feel God's power most strongly when we're in the center of His will. And where the Spirit of the Lord is, there is freedom (2 Corinthians 3:17). Freedom not to do what we want when we want it, but to *become* everything God intended us to be from the beginning of time.

My years in youth ministry revealed a soul captivity that God needed to deal with in me. He's such an efficient God! Somehow He managed to minister *through me* to the youth and minister *to me* by His Spirit. While I served Him in a way that didn't necessarily play to my strengths, it did bring my weaknesses to the surface, which created in me a deeper dependence on the Lord. And as I leaned in close, He healed something in me.

And the church leader who tried to guilt me into an un-appointed obligation? He spoke to me out of frustration because of job stresses he'd brought upon himself. Things were falling off his plate and he had lots of gaps to fill. The problem was, he'd been secretly spending his time doing things no Christian should ever do. He lived a double life, and it eventually caught up with him. And though he held a position of authority in the church (which he lost once things surfaced), he didn't represent God's heart for me when he reprimanded me. I'm so grateful I know what Jesus sounds like when He speaks.

My sheep listen to my voice; I know them, and they follow me.

John 10:27

Freedom's Invitation

When it comes to our yeses and no's, what does true freedom look like for the Christ-follower? Among other things, it means:

- We're free from the law of sin and death. We've nothing to prove. No one to impress. Our honor comes from God alone. We're already heirs (Psalm 62:7, Romans 8:2, Romans 8:17).

- It will never be about how high we can jump because He already stooped down to make us great (Psalm 18:35).

- We're called to stop our striving and straining to prove ourselves and to please others. We cannot please God if our driving motivation is to please others. We're invited to more deeply and intimately know that *He* is God (Galatians 1:10, Psalm 46:10).

- We're invited to lay hold of God's promises so we can *participate in His divine nature* and escape the world's destructive ways (2 Peter 1:4).

- We're invited to do great things during our time on this earth (John 14:12).

- We're invited to know God's love—more and more—so we will spill over with the fullness of God (Ephesians 3:19).

- We're invited to give God access to our hearts so He can do above and beyond all we could ever dare to ask or dream or imagine for His glory and for our story (Ephesians 3:20–21).

- We're invited to battle training so we can stand on high places and win one victory after another (Psalm 18).

- We're invited to pray passionately, persistently, and specifically (Matthew 7:7–8).

- We're invited to embrace feisty faith and tenacious hope amidst unfathomable odds. Overwhelming victory belongs to us because we belong to Him (Romans 8:37).

Picture yourself going out to the mailbox to get your day's mail. Amidst the stack of bills, junk mail, and countless appeals for money, you find a royal envelope with gold embossed letters and the King's wax seal on the back. You open the envelope to find a finely crafted invitation addressed personally to *you*. Your name is written in gold script, and just underneath you read these words:

The King Requests Your Presence
He invites you to become part of the royal family.
There's a place at His table for you.
He wants to redeem your story.
He wants you to be His ambassador.
You'll no longer be an orphan or a slave.
He wants to make you an heir.
All that He has will belong to you.
Come as you are.
He'll care for you and guide you every step of the way.
Please RSVP?

Do you dare trust Him? Will you say yes to the invitation to be much with God no matter what others think about the way you follow Him? Every single time you trust Him, every yes you give Him, changes *you*.

He moves on every act prompted by your faith. You're safe with Him. Loved by Him. Redeemed because of Him. You are everything to Him. Will you say yes to Him? He invites you to trust Him with your worth, your reputation, and your schedule. No more striving to manage others' opinions of you. You're no longer a slave. Let the drivers and strivers think what they want. They'll be proven wrong someday anyway. Live a redeemed life. It's the life that most fits you here and bears the most fruit for eternity. Will you trust Him?

Now picture finding an old, dirty notebook on the sidewalk. You pick it up and, to your horror, find every sin you've ever committed written on its pages. You look around to see if anybody notices as you recall your past misdeeds. It seems you can't get away from the person you used to be. You whip through the dirty pages until you get to the end of the notebook. In the back you see a statement that takes the wind right out of your sails:

> You've messed up more than most. You'll never be enough. But go ahead and try. Try hard. Maybe you'll outdo someone else and feel better about yourself. At least until someone better than you comes along. Good luck with that. Happy trying.

Notice the distinction between these two motivations:

Invitation: *a request to participate*
Obligation: *an expectation of duty*

As heirs of God who've already been saved by Christ's precious blood, what do we lose if we miss most of the daily invitations He offers us? We don't lose our salvation. We don't lose His love. So what do we lose if we bypass the invitation for the obligation? God invites us to live completely disproportionate to who we are not because He wants something from us, but because He wants something *for* us. We get to partner with God Almighty—creator of heaven and earth!

Think about that for a moment. We get to walk intimately with the God who created the universe. We get to hear His voice, receive His wisdom, see with spiritual eyes, understand the times, know the best path to take, discern how to stand in battle, and lay hold of the promised places He has offered us. We get to partner with the Lord Himself to carry out His plans on the earth.

He fills us with His Spirit, gives us access to His presence, makes us promises He intends to fulfill, and then invites us to trust Him to move mountains, part seas, and change lives.

Isn't it amazing how often we shrug our shoulders at His royal invitation and His holy declarations about our worth, and instead use our precious time and energy to keep mere humans thinking favorably of us? Lord, forgive us.

When you consider the greatness and vastness of God, it's almost laughable that we would think for a moment that our "ought-to's" and "should-do's" would accomplish anything of substance in the greater kingdom story. The following passage speaks of how we give gifts, but I think it fits for wise living as well:

> Each of you should give what you have decided in your heart to give, not reluctantly or under compulsion, for God loves a cheerful giver.
>
> 2 Corinthians 9:7

God doesn't want our halfhearted *I-suppose-I-ought-to* yes, nor does He want our *There's-no-way-out of-this-one* yes.

His invitation calls us out of captivity, not into it.

I know for myself, whenever my faith-walk becomes one of ought-to's and should-do's, it's time to step back and remember who I am and what I possess because of Christ in me. Remembering His love and His promises frees me to respond to His invitation to exercise my faith and believe Him for great things. Let's look at the difference between captivity-minded religion and freedom-minded relationship:

A captivity mindset sounds like this:

- I ought to read my Bible more; I don't do that enough.
- I ought to pray more often; I never pray enough.
- I ought to serve at church more regularly; I never serve enough.
- I ought to give more money to ministries; I never give enough.
- I ought to quit worrying so much; I always worry too much.

A freedom mindset sounds like this:

- I *get* to read Scripture with an expectancy that God will speak to me!
- I *get* to talk with God and have Him talk with me. I get to pray and see things change on earth through my prayers!
- I *get* to serve in a way that fits who God has called me to be. His grace abounds in me to do all He has called me to do!
- I *get* to obey God in ways that make no sense to me sometimes. But I can always know that He is profoundly good, and His will for me is my best-case scenario!
- I *get* to sow generously into kingdom causes that make my heart beat strong for God. I get to be part of a bigger story than my own. I get to see God supply all of my needs in a supernatural way!
- I *get* to engage my faith in a way that changes me from the inside out. I get to bring pleasure to God's heart with the way that I trust Him to be there for me. We are in this thing together!

God offered us the amazing gift of salvation through Jesus Christ. As Christians we admit that at some point in our journey, we said yes to Christ's offer of payment for our sins. That first yes to Christ was, and always will be, our most significant yes.

But from there we're offered countless opportunities to walk with Him, work with Him, and reach the world through Him.

Allow me to ask this question one more time so the truth of it will sink deep into our souls: Do all of those yeses—whether we offer them back to God or not—affect our salvation? No. Do they impact His love for us? No. Never. Nothing can separate us from His unfathomable love for us. So what's the point? Why does it matter who and what we say yes to?

Scripture seems pretty clear that some who are saved will arrive in heaven with almost nothing to show for it. They'll be saved by grace but will have little fruit to speak of, no crowns to lie at Jesus' feet. Saved with only the shirt on their backs. Read this sobering passage:

> Each one's work will become obvious, for the day will disclose it, because it will be revealed by fire; the fire will test the quality of each one's work. If anyone's work that he has built survives, he will receive a reward. If anyone's work is burned up, it will be lost, but he will be saved; yet it will be like an escape through fire.
>
> 1 Corinthians 3:13–15 HCSB

In the remaining chapters we'll unpack the meaning of this verse so we won't be one of those people whose life's work and striving efforts go up in smoke. But for now, it's important to note that when we strive in our own strength because we refuse to believe the beautiful truth about ourselves, none of those efforts will matter in the end. They'll burn up like yesterday's news.

But every time—Every. Single. Time—we choose to trust the truth about our royal status, and we live as ones who are spoken for, and we draw on the resources of heaven to accomplish God's purposes on the earth, every humble, confident response to our divine identity will change our lives, impact our world, and ripple into eternity.

The freedom God offers us is soul freedom, eternal freedom, and identity freedom. We have nothing to prove. We have only Him to please. And what pleases Him most? When we trust in His love and when we engage our faith as a holy response to our royal identity. Memorize this passage, this life-changing reminder if you can: "And without faith it is impossible to please God, because anyone who comes to him must believe that he exists and that he rewards those who earnestly seek him" (Hebrews 11:6).

Precious Lord,
Oh, how You love me! Fill me with the passion and the power of the Holy Spirit. Awaken me to my divine and royal status in You. Lord, I believe what You say about me. But when I falter, help me in my unbelief. Lead me to a rock that is higher than I. Open my eyes to the wonder of Your love, the promise of Your provision, and the power of Your promises. I want to live and breathe and serve and give as one who is spoken for. I put the fear of man under my feet and I embrace a holy reverence for You, O God. There is no one like You, Lord. You created the heavens and the earth, and You created me. Help me to live free, full of grace, abounding in love, and spilling over hope to everyone I meet. I'm not who I was. I'm not what I do. I'm someone You dearly love. May every single step I take on this earth reveal a growing knowledge of who I am in You. Thank You for taking me in and for redeeming my story. You are everything to me. Amen.

Personal Reflection

1. Can you think of a time when someone used guilt to get you to commit to something you didn't want to do? Why do you suppose their guilt tactic worked? What was going on in your heart?

2. Can you think of a time when you managed to say no—because you knew it was the right thing to do—regardless of the pressure put upon you to commit? What thought process helped you hold your ground? What was the fruit of that decision?

3. Do you have a sense of God's yes for you in this season of life? What do you have to say no to in order to give your yes to God?

4. Are there commitments on your calendar that you know shouldn't be there? Consider what drove you to say yes. Ask God for clarity around your tendency to say yes.

5. Would it be appropriate for you to remove any of those commitments from your calendar? Before you answer too quickly, ask the Lord for wisdom and peace as to the next steps you should take. It's not the worst thing in the world to admit that you overstepped and need to step back. Ask the Lord what you should do.

A *Wise Word*

The redemptive work of God in a sinner is a complete miracle. Only God can regenerate a lost soul, and only he can make that soul holy. Believing that I can somehow bring about spiritual change in my life through my hard work insults and cheapens the work of God's Spirit in me. I can't help God; only He can help me.[2]

Group Discussion Starters

1. Share about a time when you had the courage to say no to a life-draining obligation.

2. Consider the verse at the beginning of the chapter (2 Corinthians 3:17). What's the connection between the Spirit

of the Lord and our capacity for freedom? Why does freedom become a possibility when the Spirit of the Lord is allowed free rein?

3. Sometimes people pressure us to commit because of their own overcrowded life. Have you found a good answer for those who tend to pressure you because they themselves are stressed? If so, please share it with the group and offer examples of how it has worked in your life.

4. What do you sense God inviting you to do right now? Is He calling you to serve in a way that doesn't suit you? Is He calling you to say no even though some may not approve? Is He asking you to step out in faith even though you might fail? Explain.

5. Consider your life a year from now. When it comes to your life, your perspective, and your commitments, what will growth and maturity look like for you?

Faith Declaration

I declare in the mighty name of Jesus that I am an anointed, appointed child of God! I am filled with the Holy Spirit and empowered by His love. I walk in the Lord's presence as I live here on earth. I have eyes to see, ears to hear, and a heart to do His will. I refuse to throw my yes around like it doesn't matter. Life is a gift, and my time is a gift. God invites me to walk with Him and do the next thing He gives me to do. I am loved, called, and fully equipped to live the powerful life God has assigned to me. I refuse the rat race because God has called me to the sacred race. And I will run with holy passion and conviction. In Jesus' name I pray, Amen!

THE
SACRED
Yes

✤ 9 ✤

When God Redirects

Say Yes to Necessary Change

Teach us to number our days, that we may gain a
heart of wisdom.

Psalm 90:12

Time may be our scarcest and most precious re-
source. And we will begin to use it well only when
we realize we do not have an infinite supply to use.[1]

Kevin DeYoung

One day, many years ago, my husband unexpectedly came home
from work in the early afternoon. He normally worked long
days, but during this particular season, he battled cancer. Major
surgery and then radiation treatments temporarily changed the
structure of his work life.

I watched my big, strong husband grow tired, shaky, and
weak. He insisted on going to work a few hours each day prior

to his treatments. He admitted later, though, that he never accomplished much during that time.

That particular afternoon, Kevin set down his computer bag and took a few slow steps to the kitchen. He didn't look well at all.

My six-foot-three husband raked his fingers through his hair and leaned on the counter for support. He looked down at his feet and then back up at me. His eyes welled up with tears. He shook his head like he had something to say but couldn't find the words. I swallowed hard and waited for him to continue.

He finally spoke. "What are we doing? What am *I* doing?"

My words caught in my throat. "What do you mean?"

He continued, "I've been running so hard for so long, I didn't think I had another speed or gear. But this radiation has slowed me way down. I barely have the strength to get through the day.

"Then something happened on my commute home today. Traffic came to a complete stop on the highway entrance ramp. Cars lined up and people honked their horns while a lone car stalled at the bottom of the ramp.

"People swerved around the driver, honked at him, shook fists at him, exasperated at how he'd inconvenienced them. I didn't make a rude gesture, but on a normal, healthy day, it would have bothered me that this man slowed me down and interrupted my pace.

"But today I had no strength. So I waited my turn. And when I pulled up next to him, I paused to see if he was okay."

In almost thirty years of marriage, I've seen my husband cry only a handful of times. At that moment in the kitchen, he struggled to find words as he choked back his tears.

With my eyes fixed on him, I pulled myself up and sat on the kitchen counter. And held my breath. I didn't want to miss a word he had to say.

He went on, "The man at the bottom of the entrance ramp . . . he stopped there because he couldn't breathe. He's one of my radiation buddies. A sweet old man, he's battling lung cancer. He doesn't have much time to live."

He sucked in a sob and continued, "He stopped traffic and 'inconvenienced all of those people' because of a coughing fit. He was simply struggling to catch his breath."

I put my hand over my mouth because I didn't know what to say.

Kevin's lips quivered as he blinked back more tears. "What on earth have I been doing by working all these hours? And why do I think my time is more important than anyone else's? How have I missed the blessing of this life God has given me?

"I'm going to survive this cancer, but who of us really knows how many days or hours we have left on this earth? Our time has to count. I have a beautiful wife and three sons who need me."

He stepped toward me, wrapped his arms around my waist, and pulled me close. I wrapped my arms around him. We pressed our faces together and wept.

That memory will forever be etched in our hearts as one of the most sacred moments of our lives. There in that place of sickness, fatigue, and eye-opening wonder, the veil between heaven and earth seemed especially thin.

Yes Means No

Our no matters because our yes matters more. And *anytime we say yes, we say no.* If we say yes to working too many hours (beyond what God has asked of us), we say no to family and friends and the sacred life rhythm God offers us. If we say yes to serving on five committees as church, we say no to times of rest in God's presence where we receive fresh revelation from Him.

When we say yes to purchasing more items than we can afford, we say no to financial freedom and to the adventure of giving away lots of money to kingdom causes around the world. When we say yes to overindulgence—on any level—we say no to soul freedom, and we give the enemy opportunity to destroy our lives and our influence.

Furthermore, when we say yes to fear, we allow the enemy access to our lives through insecurity, doubt, and unbelief. When we say yes to the lie, we say no to the best of what God has for us: wholeness, faith, joy, expectancy, influence, fruitfulness, and changed lives all around.

Whenever we say yes, we also say no.

If we dare to assess our souls, can we honestly say that most of our yeses reveal that we know we are heirs of God? Or do our yeses make us look like the rest of the lost world?

Are we aware of how sacred and precious our time, talents, and gifts are? Do we live out of the divine supply God has offered us? Do we keep heaven busy with our prayers? Does heaven *move* because of our claim on God's promises? Or do spiritual resources remain untouched because we continually forget to look up and remember who we are and why we're here?

Why does it so often take tragedies, hardships, and heartaches to make us stop and really think about our lives to the point that we change our priorities? It's because this is how we tend to roll:

- We forget who we are.
- We race through our moments.
- We medicate our pain and discomfort.
- We forget about eternity.

Yet God calls us to live right now with eternity in mind. He knows we need reminding—time and time again—that how we live during this short time on earth deeply impacts how we'll live out our eternity. Life on earth is short. Eternity is long.

Remember what we talked about in chapter 7? We're small. God is great. And spiritual activity swirls all around us. But we miss the essence of our importance and God's presence when we spend and waste time as if we've an endless supply of time to draw from. We don't.

None of us knows how many days or moments we have left to live. But what we do have is an ever-present God to guide us every step of the way. He knows the best way for us. He knows that when we live and give and pray in faith, we'll change the world and reap a harvest in heaven. He also knows that when we drive and strive and race through life, we miss the sacredness of the moment, the needs around us, and the opportunity to invest in our eternity.

God will use anything and everything in our lives to get us to look up that we might see our lives and ourselves from His point of view. He'll even use the hardships the enemy sends our way to jar us awake. He'd rather we gain ground in our trials than lose ground in our slumber.

And though we mourn and struggle through the pain of it all, we must also consider our pain a sacred gift from a heavenly Father who—more than anything—wants our life to count for eternity.

What "thin veil" moments have you experienced in your life? Can you think of a time or two when God used pain or discomfort to help you reset your course and look up?

R. T. Kendall writes:

> When you sense that God is trying to get your attention, it is because He *is* indeed trying to get your attention. If, therefore, as you read these lines you can sense that God is calling for you, then be glad and rejoice; you have a future. But *you must not assume you will feel this way tomorrow.* Today is the day of salvation (see 2 Corinthians 6:2). Thank God for any slap on the wrist, any sense of warning. It means you have a future. God always shows a way forward when we are open to His will. Wisdom is knowing the next step forward; God will show you the next thing to do.[2]

Many years ago I realized that my tendency to overcommit—even to really good things—had driven me to utter exhaustion. I took out a piece of paper and a pen, and I wrote down every one of my time commitments and obligations. When I finished, I stared at the overly long list before me.

My friend and I put our hands on the paper, bowed our heads, and I prayed, "These commitments before me, Lord, are You still blessing them? Are You still asking me to give my time in these ways? Is there anything on this list I need to gracefully bow out of? Is there anything on this list that I need to devote more time to? Search me, God, and know my heart; test me and know my anxious thoughts. See if there is any offensive way in me, and lead me in the way everlasting" (Psalm 139:23–24).

Then I waited. And God spoke to me. In a relatively short amount of time He provided clarity on some life adjustments I needed to make.

Some of His insights surprised me, others not so much. If I'm honest, I have to own the fact that the winds of change had been blowing for some time regarding a couple of my commitments. However, I feared to make the move—afraid I'd inconvenience others, afraid of how it would look to back out now, and afraid I'd gotten myself into something that would be difficult to get out of. So I conveniently ignored the breeze blowing through my hair and reasoned that God had intended those winds of change for somebody else, like my busy husband.

Here's the thing: either we heed those gentle warnings from the Holy Spirit, or we continue on a lifeless path of striving and straining, and eventually crash and burn. The Lord sees the gap in the train track up ahead and wants to protect us. But we must trust Him enough to listen to Him, even when it seems it could cost us in the short run to stop the speeding train we're on.

Remember, life on earth is short, and eternity is long. Our goal—as Christ-followers—is to live and move and breathe with eternity in mind.

Time to Make a Change?

A doctor friend of mine once said to another friend, "Just because God directs you to go to nursing school doesn't mean He intends for you to become a nurse." Think about that for a moment. Just because God connected the dots for you to meet a certain man or woman doesn't mean He intends for you to marry that person. Just because God led you to start a ministry to the homeless, or to women, or to children doesn't mean He intends for you to oversee that particular ministry until you die.

It's far too easy to presume upon God and go on autopilot when it comes to our commitments. We reason that since God first led us to this place, it's okay for us to give away one yes after another without thinking too much about it. And when we suddenly hit a wall of burnout, we wonder how it happened. Or we have a relational blowup that could have been avoided had we made our exit when we first sensed God's direction to move or make a change.

Far too often we continue to say yes long after God's grace for the task has lifted. He's moved us on, but for some reason we're still there. An old saint named Bob Mumford once told a pastor friend of ours, "When the horse is dead, it's time to dismount."

Do you feel the winds of change starting to blow? If you sense the Lord urging you to move, and you sense the grace has lifted, you'd best be on your way.

We do unnecessary damage to our health and our relationships when we postpone our obedience. Plus, when we stay longer than we should, we fill a slot and take up space where God intends to bring fresh life through somebody else.

Though there are seasons of rest and seasons to run, God's call *never* includes cruise control. When we go on autopilot and run from one thing to the next without much thought, we disengage our faith and hearts until we no longer hear God's voice clearly, which makes us dull to the gentle nudges of the Holy Spirit.

Just because God led us to a particular place years ago doesn't mean He won't lead us on from that place when His best will requires it. While there's great virtue in being faithful where God has us, it is equally important that we keep an ear bent toward heaven so we will hear and recognize His gentle whisper nudging us, *This is the way, walk ye in it.*

The Lord reserves the right to interrupt our plans, call us out of commitments, and engage us in ways that defy our sensibilities. This is what it means to trust Him with our whole hearts and not rely so heavily on our own understanding.

Can I ask you a few soul-searching questions?

What saps the life from you these days? What drains you dry? Do you continue to give your time to something that you know just isn't good for you in this particular season of life? Mind if I continue? How's it working for you? Are you tired enough yet? Ready for a change? Read these wise words from Dr. Henry Cloud:

> The first step that will motivate you to do what is necessary is to see that what you are doing has no hope of getting what you want. When that happens, you will instantly feel an epiphany. You realize that to get where you want to get, you *must* make a change. You really get it that to continue to do what you are doing is hopeless, and then you will begin to see motivation to make change appear. So hopelessness can bring us closer to fearlessness, as *it does not take courage to stop doing what you know is not going to work.*[3]

I've noticed that the longer we stay with something beyond the time that God has urged us to go, the more the commitment takes out of us and the more it costs those around us. God seems to offer us a window of time—a window of grace to move from one thing to the next. He knows we're often slow to adapt. But once that window closes, we lose steam fast and we wonder why things feel so hard. And the longer we dig in our heels and try to make it work—outside of God's will for us—the more severe the burnout tends to be and the longer it takes us to recover from such an un-anointed output of our energy and time.

Remember this: Even Jesus, the Son of God, relied heavily on His Father for every word He spoke and every step He took. We're wise to follow in His footsteps.

Should I Stay or Should I Go?

We tend to make two common mistakes: We either stay too long or we quit too soon. Here's an important side note: Just because something is hard and feels life draining doesn't mean it's outside of God's will for us in that particular season. I can think of a number of commitments that felt like they'd kill me if I didn't pull out of them. I begged God to release me, and He wouldn't.

Now, looking back, I can see how those chapters of my life prepared me for the road ahead. And I praise Him for helping me hang in there because I developed some grit in my faith. Better yet, I gained a few lifelong relationships that I'd probably not have right now had I left prior to God's timing for me.

How do we know if we're supposed to stay or go? We seek God's face daily. We listen for His voice. And we follow His lead.

Sometimes He calls us to stay when we'd rather go. In those times, the necessary change needs to be *within us*. Our pastor often says, "You're not free to go until you're free to stay." Believe it or not, it's possible to experience a soul-revival in a season of life that we absolutely hate, one that we're desperate to be delivered from. Oftentimes it takes just a shift of perspective and a change of heart to see God's provision and even protection in a place where we do not want to be. What are the first steps we need to take during such a time?

- Surrender our will: *"Therefore, I urge you, brothers and sisters, in view of God's mercy, to offer your bodies as a living sacrifice, holy and pleasing to God—this is your true and proper worship"* (Romans 12:1).
- Change our perspective: *"Do not conform to the pattern of this world, but be transformed by the renewing of your mind. Then you will be able to test and approve what God's will is—his good, pleasing and perfect will"* (Romans 12:2).
- Give thanks and worship: *"Give thanks in all circumstances; for this is God's will for you in Christ Jesus"* (1 Thessalonians 5:18).
- Live with expectancy: *"I remain confident of this: I will see the goodness of the Lord in the land of the living"* (Psalm 27:13).

Other times He calls us to go when we'd rather stay. We may love what we're doing and we may see fruitfulness all around, and God's direction to leave may make absolutely no sense to us, but He knows what's best for us. We can trust Him. How do we dare take the faith steps before us when we'd rather stay put?

- We trust Him more than we trust ourselves: *"Trust God from the bottom of your heart; don't try to figure out everything on your own. Listen for God's voice in everything you do, everywhere you go; he's the one who will keep you on track. Don't assume that you know it all"* (Proverbs 3:5–6 THE MESSAGE).
- We refuse the temptation to worry and be anxious: *"Do not be anxious about anything, but in every situation, by prayer and petition, with thanksgiving, present your requests to God. And the peace of God, which transcends all understanding, will guard your hearts and your minds in Christ Jesus"* (Philippians 4:6–7).

- We prioritize spending time with Him: *"And without faith it is impossible to please God, because anyone who comes to him must believe that he exists and that he rewards those who earnestly seek him"* (Hebrews 11:6).
- We keep a firm grip on His promises to us: *"Let us hold unswervingly to the hope we profess, for he who promised is faithful"* (Hebrews 10:23).

Fresh Wind in Your Sails

What do we miss out on when we're shackled to our commitments or even our own reasoning because we don't have the courage to make the necessary adjustments that God so wisely has for us?

We miss out on the best of God's power, grace, and peace. All too often we prefer a known captivity to an unknown freedom. But there's freedom in God's yes. He supplies peace and power and all of the grace we need to walk in faith and to live in a way that changes things on earth and impacts our eternity. Just this morning I read these words from one of my favorite devotionals, *Streams in the Desert*:

> The Lord imparts to me the underlying strength of character that gives me the necessary energy and decision-making ability to live my life. He strengthens me "with power through his Spirit in (my) inner being" (Eph. 3:16). And the strength He gives is continuous, for He is a source of power I cannot exhaust. "Your strength will equal your days" (Deut. 33:25)—my strength of will, affection, judgment, ideals, and achievement will last a lifetime. "The Lord is my strength" (Ex. 15:2) *to go on.*[4]

The other day I had lunch with my friend Stephanie. She works a steady job, owns a townhome, and has—for a while now—felt the winds of change moving in her life. How did she respond to this inner restlessness? She grabbed her Bible. She pressed in and prayed; she leaned in and listened, and then she did the next thing God nudged her to do.

By the time we met for lunch, she had a number of life-changing decisions to share with me. Risky ones. Exciting steps, but scary too. And I could tell by the look in her eyes and the peace in her spirit that she's right in step with her Savior.

I got so excited about what the Lord's been saying to Stephanie, I pulled out my phone and took notes on our conversation. Read the words of a woman who dares to follow God's lead. Notice how her faith steps have impacted her perspective, her peace, and her sense of soul freedom:

> I got so tired of feeling stuck that I finally had to ask myself: What *is* it that I'm holding on so tightly to that I'm not seeing what God wants to show me? And not hearing what God is trying to say to me? For me, it's *not* been a sacred yes; it's been a self-righteous, self-preserving yes . . . a seemingly safe yes, but it's *not* been safe. I've been held captive by my own self-protection. In fact, saying yes to God's yes even involves risk. But that's what we're made for, where life is. I'm hearing Him now, and it's so exhilarating, adventurous, and freeing. I know I'm right where He wants me to be. His peace is in me and on me. I don't know what's up ahead for me, but I know that these are the next steps I'm supposed to take. I will trust Him. And I feel fully alive in it all!

Can you sense the passion in her soul? Don't you want that for yourself? Part of what it means to embrace a sacred yes is simply to give our *next* yes to God. And then give Him the yes after that, and then the yes after that. Whatever He tells you to do, do it. Whatever He asks of you, trust Him; He'll see you through it.

God is so very good and loves you so very much. It's time to redeem your time. Don't wait for a tragedy to remember that life is a gift, your walk is sacred, and there's a God in heaven who loves you deeply and knows—better than you—what's best for you. We inhabit this earth for such a short yet important time. How we live here determines how we'll live there, on the other side. May we live as ones who are spoken for.

Precious Lord,

Teach me to number my days, that I may grow in the knowledge of You and gain a heart of wisdom! May Your love abound in me more and more. May I increase daily in all wisdom, knowledge, and depth of insight. May I understand the times and know what to do. Help me to highly discern Your will and Your ways that I may live daily in step with You. Open my spirit-eyes and help me to redeem my moments for eternity. May I be fully aware of Your movement in and all around me. I want to be sensitive to Your nudges to move on when you tell me to, and I want to trust You when You call me to stay. You know what's best for me and I trust You with my whole heart. Fill me afresh with the wonder of Your love and the power of Your Name. Help me to be the anointed, appointed child of God You always intended me to be. In Your precious name I pray. Amen.

Personal Reflection

1. What experiences in your life has God used to get your attention? What was His message to you?

2. Did that message stick with you? Did you make a course change, or did you forget about it over time? Why or why not?

3. Can you think of a time in your life when you stayed too long or left too soon?

4. What was the impact or the cost to you and to others? What did you learn?

5. Is God nudging you right now—to either make a change or change your perspective? What are your next steps?

A *Wise Word*

We've got Jesus. We've got the all-glorious Son of God. Let's keep whispering the news to each other so none of us will miss him. Everything he is, everything he's done, everything he possesses, all belongs *to us*. He's right here with us in this moment, pouring out grace upon grace, and up ahead is that glorious day when we'll finally see him face to face. We've got Jesus and he's got us.[5]

Group Discussion Starters

1. Share about a time when God used a circumstance or hardship to get your attention and give you a fresh perspective.

2. When you consider the two common mistakes we often make—staying too long or leaving too soon—which of these are you more prone to do? Explain.

3. Recall a time when you either left too soon or stayed too long, and share the circumstances surrounding the situation and the impact of your decision.

4. What hardship or trial has already produced a certain glory in your life (e.g., my husband said that though he never wants to go through cancer again, he wouldn't trade it for the world)? Does this experience compel you to view your other trials differently?

5. In what ways do you sense God asking you to more intentionally engage your faith?

Faith Declaration

I declare in the mighty name of Jesus that I am an anointed, appointed child of God! I am filled with the Holy Spirit and empowered by His love. I walk in the Lord's presence as I live here on earth. I have eyes to see, ears to hear, and a heart to do His will. I refuse to throw my yes around like it doesn't matter. Life is a gift, and my time is a gift. God invites me to walk with Him and do the next thing He gives me to do. I am loved, called, and fully equipped to live the powerful life God has assigned to me. I refuse the rat race because God has called me to the sacred race. And I will run with holy passion and conviction. In Jesus' name I pray, Amen!

❖ 10 ❖

Simple Sacred Steps

Say Yes to Divine Momentum

But what happens when we live God's way? He brings gifts into our lives, much the same way that fruit appears in an orchard—things like affection for others, exuberance about life, serenity. We develop a willingness to stick with things, a sense of compassion in the heart, and a conviction that a basic holiness permeates things and people. We find ourselves involved in loyal commitments, not needing to force our way in life, able to marshal and direct our energies wisely.

Galatians 5:22–23 THE MESSAGE

We must place God at the center of all things, and build outward from there, rationally and consistently. . . . Making our choices in the light of accepted limits, we reassess regularly and defend each area of importance against the onslaught of other demands.[1]

Dr. Richard Swenson

In this chapter I want to talk about the power of consistency in our lives. I strongly believe that you can't get the most out of life—or honor the Lord with your whole self—without practicing certain disciplines.

But before I talk about this, I want to make sure I emphasize what I'm *not* saying. First, this isn't about God loving you any more for all your hard work for Him. He already loves you more than you know, and what you do will not change that. Second, disciplines look very different for different people. Let me tell you about my friend Sandy to show you what I mean. . . .

Last summer I enjoyed one of the best bike rides of my life. I know I've already mentioned this, but I love to cycle. I especially love to ride the bike trails as fast as I can for miles at a time. The hotter the day, the better for me.

This particular day I rode about thirty miles at a steady fast pace. I climbed hills aggressively, enjoyed some coasting recovery time, and took in the beauty all around me. The sun burned brightly—not a cloud in the sky. It was a hot, wonderfully humid day. Soaked with sweat, my ponytail dripped down my back. My shins covered in dirt, I smiled big as I hoisted my bike back onto its rack. I felt glorious by the end of that ride. Fully alive and profoundly grateful, I thanked the Lord for such a life-giving adventure.

My dear friend Sandy considers this kind of experience right up there with root canals or cleaning the garage. She loves to ride, but she's not fond of extreme heat and doesn't enjoy cycling at a sprint pace. She'd rather go slow—very slow—painfully slow for me. She doesn't want to miss the birds fluttering through the meadow. She likes to get off her bike and chase butterflies.

Riding with her makes me want to take a nap. We both deeply love Jesus, both love to exercise, and really love each other. But instead of biking together, we go out to eat, or we swim, or we sit and talk until we giggle and snort.

What makes her come alive and what makes me come alive are mostly different things. She likes novels that take their time to develop. I like novels that move so fast I forget to breathe.

She's most alive and productive late at night. Or in the middle of the night. My personality makes a hasty exit at about 9:00 p.m. She loves spontaneity and a loosely based plan. I love structure, routine, plan A, and plan B. Ironically, she likes fast speedboats and I love slow pontoon rides. We're different that way too.

But we have this in common: We see life as a precious, sacred gift from God, and we want every moment to matter. God loves that He made us different, and loves even more how richly connected we are because of *Him*.

My friend knows how to nourish her soul, nurture her heart, and care for the things that matter in her life. I know how that looks for me too. And yet as you can imagine, our paths look very different from one another.

We both understand that it's not about how we pray, but *that* we pray. It's not about how we exercise, it's *that* we exercise. It's not about how we give and live and rest and get replenished—it's *that* we do.

We both find life in God's yes for us. When we follow His lead, our steps become sacred, our tasks turn into offerings, and our battles, we learn, are winnable. But His yes for you will be different from His yes for me. Obedience for you may be disobedience for me, depending on the seasons of life we're in.

Walking in God's yes for us calls for faith and flexibility, engagement and expectancy, awareness and alertness. The more consistently we engage our hearts and do what He says, the more spiritually agile and fit we become. We'll navigate change more easily. We'll carry our burdens differently. And we'll love more freely. Jesus uses our everyday moments to train us for battle and to transform us into His likeness.

But if we placed your journey and my journey side by side, they might look very different, because He has purposely wired us different from each other. Your life-giving journey fits *you*.

Another friend of mine, Susan, explained it this way:

> I think our true selves—our true fit—*will* make sense to us. It will feel right. It will feel full of life. It will make us feel safe and loved for who we are. Doing something that doesn't make sense is not necessarily wisdom or faith or good for our souls. Life-giving and life-sustaining results come from attention and intention—from the invitation.

God's call for you is available, accessible. Your call is to discern it.

The Power of Consistency

However, regardless of your personality type or season of life, a certain measure of consistency is essential for anyone who wants to live a strong, stable, fruitful life. Again, it's not how we do these disciplines, it's *that* we do them. Walking in God's yes for us calls for *diligence with the things that matter*—if we truly want to abound in every good thing God has for us.

Diligence *is* man's precious possession (Proverbs 12:27 NKJV). My mentor says that diligence is the art of steady application, and steady application creates forward movement that gains strength with time.

We tend to think of disciplines as a list of ought-to's and should do's, as acts of legalism borne out of our need to feel spiritual. And the truth is, they *can* be when we implement them for the wrong reasons.

But when we look to the Lord for strength, motivation, and inspiration, and when we begin to see the cumulative effect that our life-giving choices offer us, we'll see how our small yet regular efforts reap a harvest of results in our lives. Always remember this: God *wants* to empower us to do what's absolutely best for us. Read this passage: "For God is working in you, giving you the desire and the power to do what pleases him" (Philippians 2:13 NLT).

Everywhere we place our feet, every habit we embrace, reveals what we believe about God and ourselves. We're made for spiritual progress—to move forward into maturity, to journey onward, to grow more and more like Christ as we travel toward our heavenly home.

We're not called to perfection. We won't get it right all the time. We're covered in grace—but not a grace that calls for slothful ease or frantic effort. It's a grace that invites us to rest in the finished work of Christ *and* to be empowered to live in a way that far exceeds our ability and capacity for greatness and godliness. Scripture says, "'For in him we live and move and have our being.' As some of your own poets have said, 'We are his offspring'" (Acts 17:28).

We are made by God and for God, that we might walk with God and live from the strength, energy, and power He provides. The Lord wired us for forward progress, spiritual traction, abundant fruit, and an increasing knowledge of God.

Yet without even realizing it, we subtly let go of the little things, the important things that gird us up, give us strength, and keep us moving forward into the best of what God has for us.

Think about how inconsistency impacts us in everyday life:

- The youth group kid who never feels accepted, included, or like a valid member of the group because of her random and occasional attendance

- The husband and wife who feel disconnected from each other because of their inconsistent efforts to prioritize their marriage
- The number on the scale that never goes down because of inconsistent boundaries on food
- The energy level that never seems to rise because there's no rhythm, routine, or consistency to the bedtime routine
- The spiritual traction that falters because of inconsistent attempts to develop a steady, sturdy devotional life
- Deep desires that never come to fruition because of only random attempts at prayer, obedience, and faith-filled risk-taking
- The missed adventure and lack of growth in generosity because of inconsistency with finances, tithing, sowing, and reaping
- The important books that never get read because of random and runaway time spent on the Internet

Dr. Wiersbe writes:

As we feed on the Word of God and apply it in daily life, our inner "spiritual senses" get their exercise and become strong and keen. . . . It is impossible to stand still in the Christian life: we either go forward and claim God's blessing, or we go backward and wander aimlessly.[2]

Now, before I go a step further, let me affirm something here. You and I? We're not who we once were and we're not what we do. We're someone Jesus loves and enjoys.

If you feel—after reading through this list—any condemnation whatsoever, know this: It's not from the Lord (nor from me).

Whenever we sense condemnation for what we miss, for not doing enough, we've got to reset our thought process and remind ourselves that we have every right to *rest in* and *rely on* the finished work of Christ. We cannot add anything to what Jesus has already achieved for us. Isn't that just the best news?

But all too often, once we cast off the condemnation, we forget to consider the invitation. When the enemy comes at us with condemnation or obligation, we must turn our backs on him and turn to Jesus.

First, put the condemnation under your feet and stomp on it. Memorize this wonderful, powerful verse: "Therefore, there is now no condemnation for those who are in Christ Jesus" (Romans 8:1).

Next, reaffirm your value and standing with Christ.

Then, lift your chin and let Jesus speak to you about what He has for you. If He issues an invitation to pray with more fervency, or to give with more hilarity (abundantly and generously), or to share the gospel more courageously, or to care for your health with more consistency, it's because He has a next-place-of-promise for you that requires it. And He will supply the power to do those things in a sustainable way. Read this passage again: "For God is working in you, giving you the desire and the power to do what pleases him" (Philippians 2:13 NLT).

Don't allow the weight of condemnation to bury you or bully you. Be lifted up by God's loving, empowering invitation. And get excited about the next thing He has for you.

God's spiritual laws appear all around us in the natural realm. Look at the farmer or the gardener. The laws of sowing, reaping, planting, and weeding apply directly to biblical concepts we read about in Scripture. Jesus calls us to steward the gifts He gives us. Things like money, gifts, opportunities, health, time, and His Word. What we sow is what we grow. Read *The Message* paraphrase of Galatians 6:7–10:

> Don't be misled: No one makes a fool of God. What a person plants, he will harvest. The person who plants selfishness, ignoring the needs of others—ignoring God!—harvests a crop

of weeds. All he'll have to show for his life is weeds! But the one who plants in response to God, letting God's Spirit do the growth work in him, harvests a crop of real life, eternal life. So let's not allow ourselves to get fatigued doing good. At the right time we will harvest a good crop if we don't give up, or quit. Right now, therefore, every time we get the chance, let us work for the benefit of all, starting with the people closest to us in the community of faith.

It's just true. Whether we like it or not, our private choices eventually bear public fruit. The things we prioritize from day to day are like seeds we plant in the ground. In due time they surface and bear fruit in our lives—good, bad, and otherwise. Though we're saved by grace and loved unconditionally, our stewardship matters to God.

Scripture has plenty to say about diligence and perseverance. God blesses and rewards the one who is righteously diligent with the things that matter because it's a physical and spiritual law, it's good practice for us, and it creates forward movement in our lives.

If we take simple, sacred steps each day—more often than not—we will acquire strength and fruit in our lives. Some of that fruit we'll see in this life and some we'll see more gloriously in the next.

Below you'll find a few examples of sacred steps that gather power and momentum over time. Some of these disciplines will require an adjustment to your day, others just a different focus. But each of these simple, life-giving choices can become an eternal investment when offered with a heart of faith. They're important steps. Easy to do. And just as easy *not* to.

- Spend daily time with God
- Study His Word
- Worship passionately

155

- Recapture a sense of awe in God's goodness, presence, and power
- Pray specifically
- Give generously
- Be thankful
- Obey God immediately
- Engage your faith
- Drink more water
- Practice restraint (regularly say no to yourself and make yourself deal with it)
- Schedule exercise
- Schedule rest
- Schedule play time
- Work diligently at your God-given tasks
- Establish a consistent bedtime routine
- Stretch your muscles
- Stand up straight
- Humble yourself
- Forgive (start with forgiving yourself)
- Forgive again
- Love your loved ones
- Love your enemies
- Kiss your kids
- Kiss your spouse
- Laugh out loud
- Take yourself less seriously
- Take God more seriously
- Ask for the impossible
- Refuse condemnation

- Reject rejection
- Accept God's acceptance
- Ask the Holy Spirit to empower and awaken you
- Remember who you are
- Remember Whose you are
- Stay in step with Jesus

Accumulative Power

Do you know someone who currently enjoys momentum in his or her life from years of diligence in his or her particular area of interest? Maybe they've applied themselves in finances, fitness, a musical instrument, or their career. While others indulged however and whenever they wanted to, this person said no to excess so they could say yes to their convictions. Whether they practiced diligence for the right reasons or not, the fruit of their discipline and the momentum of their choices is usually undeniable.

In the same way and even more important, I believe it's possible for Christ followers to experience an accumulative power and anointing in their lives simply from walking with God consistently, one sacred step at a time.

I've seen it again and again: a power, consistency, and depth present in the lives of those who—with one foot in front of the other—steadily walk with God, trust Him, spend time with Him, and do what He says.

People who've walked faithfully and consistently with God tend to possess a holy confidence and humble dependence that runs deep. They have a rootedness about them. They're grounded in God's Word. They trust Him more than they trust themselves. They're humble, teachable, gentle, but not insecure. They care far more about the needs of others than they do about what their critics have to say about them. They determined a

long time ago that the favor of God trumps popularity with
man any day of the week. They may blend in with the crowd
but they stand out from heaven's point of view. If you judged
them by the world's standard, you may miss them. But heaven
knows who's who in the zoo.

Scripture says:

- God rewards those who diligently seek after Him (Hebrews 11:6).
- He rewards publicly those who passionately pray privately (Matthew 6:6).
- He draws near to those who draw near to Him (James 4:8).
- He confides in those who fear Him (Psalm 25:14).
- Those who wait on the Lord eventually rise up and defy the gravity of their circumstances (Isaiah 40:31).

First Corinthians 1:5 says, "For in Him you have been enriched
in every way—with all kinds of speech and with all knowledge."
Here's how Rick Renner unpacks this passage:

The word "enriched" is the Greek word *plousios*, which describes *extreme or vast material wealth*. In fact, the word *plousios* is where we get the term "plutocrat," referring to a person who is so prosperous that he is unable to ascertain the full extent of his own wealth. Because his investments, his companies, and the percentage of interest he earns on his portfolio all grow so rapidly, it is impossible for his accountants and bookkeepers to keep track of how much wealth he actually possesses. . . . Because the word *plousios* is used, this verse conveys the following idea: *You are invested with great spiritual riches because you are in Him, and that's not all! The longer you remain in Him, you just keep getting blessed with more and more wealth that comes from being in Him* . . . these spiritual riches are yours by virtue of your relationships with Jesus.[3]

This idea helped me immensely during a particularly tough week many years ago. Try as I did to prepare for an upcoming speaking event with diligence and faithfulness, I just couldn't. Sick children, a broken dryer, sleepless nights, and my own frustrating health challenges snatched every last moment of my time.

Panic rose up within me because I'd answered an invitation I felt strongly was from the Lord, but then I wasn't able to do the work required to prepare for the event. I felt sure that I was about to fail God, the women who booked me, and the audience who would hear me speak. Weak, exhausted, and empty, I cried out to God for help.

His encouragement surprised me. He whispered these words to my heart: *Susie, I know you're diligent in the things that matter. You're not one to shirk responsibility. But right now, your primary responsibility is at home. Take care of your kids. Take care of yourself. I'll take care of the event. We've walked together for a long time. You have a deep well within you. Don't think for a moment that the chaos of this week disqualifies you from bringing a message this weekend. The opposite is true. Your well is deep because our relationship is real. You know who I am. I know who you are. Walk by faith. Draw from all that I've given you. I will be with You. All will be well.*

And it was. We had a powerful weekend. God's strength trumped my weakness. My years of walking with God upstaged and overpowered that week of sleepless nights. Jesus filled me up and poured me out. Women met with God. And He was glorified.

God is greater than my circumstances. He's strong in me. And He's strong in you too.

The enemy can turn us upside down when we have a bad week. But that's when we need to remember that our footing is secure in Christ. We carry a richness in our soul acquired from the miles we've traveled through life with Him.

Our spiritual wealth? It's constantly accruing—there is an accumulative anointing for the one who remains in Christ.

And just to clarify: God doesn't love the diligent person more than the one who never hits his or her stride. The diligent one isn't more saved than the one who constantly starts and stops. And Jesus shows no favorites. Just because we walk with God for many years, it doesn't mean we're less accountable—in any way—before God. Actually, we're more accountable.

Here's another crucial point: We must not confuse resting on our laurels with walking intimately with God. If we rely on our past victories, we'll fail in our current battles. However, if we rest in God more than we trust ourselves—because we have a history with Him—He'll cover us, equip us, empower us, and protect us whether we feel up for the battle or not.

I believe God consistently and profoundly uses those who daily walk with Him, who practice regular spiritual disciplines, who make it a practice to renew their minds with thoughts consistent with Scripture.

Jesus uses those who say yes with sincere and earnest hearts because they've positioned themselves to hear from God, they've made space in their lives to move with Him, and they've prioritized obedience to Him as the highest order of the day.

Have you met a person who seems to possess an accumulative, spiritual anointing and wealth from walking faithfully with God for many years and many moments in a row? That's the kind of power-in-consistency that God wants for all of us. This isn't a personality bent—it's a kingdom invitation for all who belong to God.

Travel Light

We cannot address disciplines and diligence without saying a quick word about our physical health. The world has made an idol out of our physical appearance, our bodies, and even our fitness abilities. Perhaps that's why many Christians see *any* efforts toward health and fitness as idolatrous.

As God's chosen people, we know that for us, the treasure is within. Since we are His temple, though, it matters that we care for our earthly bodies while we have them.

Unbelievers look at us and wonder why we rant so about other excesses but often indulge in food to the point that we're sick with disease.

We cannot control all things related to our health. Godly, healthy people get sick and die. But simple, basic disciplines can strengthen us to serve with energy and vitality. Our health becomes less of a hindrance to serving God and enjoying life when we give it a little attention each and every day. The smallest steps can make the biggest difference.

That being said, on our healthiest, strongest day, we remain fragile jars of clay. We're a wisp of a vapor that might be here today and gone tomorrow. We must remember that though it matters that we steward our health, our relationships, and the things entrusted to us by God, at the end of the day, we're still deeply and profoundly dependent on God. The very breath in our lungs is a gift from God. We need Him every moment of every hour.

It matters that we care for these important things that God has entrusted to us. We do our best and we leave the rest with Him. We strengthen ourselves as much as it depends on us, then we entrust ourselves to God because everything depends on Him.

I once heard author and pastor Francis Frangipane express that the Christian life is one of conquering and surrendering. We conquer the land God has put before us, and then we humbly bow low and surrender it back to Him. I love that insight and believe it to be completely true. God shows us our next place of promise. He trains us to take the land. And once we do, we bow low and *offer it back to Him.* And we rise up ready for our next assignment. We travel light because our treasure is in heaven. All of who we are and what we do is an offering to the God who saved us for His purposes.

He trains our hands for battle. He teaches us to stand on high places. He strengthens us to bend a bow of bronze. He equips us to face down our giants. He helps us overcome our fears. He leads us by still waters.

He turns us into mighty warriors yet still loves us like we're His precious, vulnerable children. Because that is what we are.

He's known all along who and what He was getting when He received us into His family. He trains us, teaches us, refines us, and heals us. He pulls us close and loves us deeply. He sends us out and uses us in ways that far exceed our wildest expectations. And when our time here is through, He intends to get us safely home.

Precious Lord,

Ignite a powerful, spiritual momentum in my life! Increase my capacity for You! Help me to grow in my knowledge and comprehension of Your Word. Empower me to pray with bold conviction and to speak with holy precision. Awaken my heart to love what You love and to see what You see. Help me to be consistent with the things that matter most in my life. Motivate me to steward the gifts and opportunities You've set before me. May I abound in love and increase daily in all wisdom, knowledge, and depth of insight. May I understand the times and know what to do. Surround me with Your favor as with a shield. Tuck me in the shadow of Your wing—teach me to dwell there, to live from that place of power and protection. May Your favor matter far more to me than man's opinion. Teach me Your way that I might walk the high path You've established for me. More, more, more of You in me, on me, and through me, Lord! My soul waits for You. Amen.

Personal Reflection

1. If you were to take inventory of your most consistent thought patterns and your most consistent choices from the past few months, what kind of pattern do they reveal? What statement do they make about your perspective on God, time, and your life?

2. Would you say that this most recent pattern in your life is consistent with your heartfelt convictions? What adjustments do you need to make?

3. In what areas of life have you taken enough consistent steps that you now see a momentum in your life? In what ways have you benefited from your consistent choices (e.g., work, marriage, recreation, health, hobby)?

4. Jesus invites you to a new and next place with Him. When He calls us to someplace new, we oftentimes need to make an adjustment in our lives. What do you sense is His invitation to you right now (e.g., to rest more and worry less; exercise more and watch less TV; pray more and talk less)? Refuse the enemy's condemnation. Get excited about God's invitation.

5. Picture yourself a year from now. Where do you want to be in your walk with God, your physical health, and your relationships with others? Is there anything in your life that you've "conquered" that you now need to surrender back to Jesus? Prayerfully consider the various aspects of this question. Invite Jesus to join you and offer His perspective here.

A *Wise Word*

It's not wrong to be tired. It's not wrong to feel overwhelmed. It's not wrong to go through seasons of complete chaos. What is wrong—and heartbreakingly foolish and wonderfully avoidable—is to live a life with more craziness than we want because we have less of Jesus than we need.[4]

Group Discussion Starters

1. Who do you know who enjoys a certain momentum in their lives? Share what you've observed about their choices.

2. In what areas of life are you most consistent? And most inconsistent?

3. What fruit do you see from your diligence in that particular area?

4. Is there an area of your life where it's hard to imagine diligence, momentum, and forward movement? Explain.

5. What simple sacred steps do you sense God wants you to take in the days ahead?

Faith Declaration

I declare in the mighty name of Jesus that I am an anointed, appointed child of God! I am filled with the Holy Spirit and empowered by His love. I walk in the Lord's presence as I live here on earth. I have eyes to see, ears to hear, and a heart to do His will. I refuse to throw my yes around like it doesn't matter. Life is a gift, and my time is a gift. God invites me to walk with Him and do the next thing

He gives me to do. I am loved, called, and fully equipped to live the powerful life God has assigned to me. I refuse the rat race because God has called me to the sacred race. And I will run with holy passion and conviction. In Jesus' name I pray, Amen!

🕸 11 🕸

Stand in Power

Say Yes to Your God-Given Influence

But to as many as did receive *and* welcome Him,
He gave the authority (power, privilege, right) to
become the children of God, that is, to those who
believe in (adhere to, trust in, and rely on) His name.

John 1:12 AMP

You've gazed at people, problems, failures, and
fears long enough. God blesses intimacy with Him
and rewards us with Himself and everything else
pertaining to life and godliness (see Hebrews 11:6;
2 Peter 1:3). Problems are changed in His presence.[1]

William L. Ford, III

Something powerful happens when we begin to align our lives
with God's yes for us. We start to enjoy the freedom to say no.
We're more careful about where we invest our time. We make

time and space to be with the Lord, to rest in His presence, and to hear His voice—which is life-giving in itself.

Life in God's yes has a rhythm to it—an ebb and flow that allows for times of running and times of resting. God assigns us a portion of His burden, not the whole weight of it. We don't have to be all things to all people or tend to every cause that's before us. We're not built for that.

The yoke He assigns to us actually makes us stronger as we go. It makes us wiser, deeper, and even richer in Christ Jesus. Walking out His best purposes for us suits us perfectly. He knows what we need, He cares deeply about our hearts, and He intends to finish in us what He started.

How do we maintain the humble confidence to say no to un-appointed work without shame, regret, or self-awareness?

By walking intimately with God. By continually seeing ourselves as personally and profoundly loved and cared for—and at the same time, as part of the bigger kingdom story.

We embrace the God-given vision for our lives—and we see this as our sacred duty: to guard our hearts and lives as ones who are set apart for Him.

Though we may battle weariness on occasion, God's yes for us will not grind our gears, wear us out, or keep us running at a sprint as a way of life. Jesus doesn't want to burn us out; He wants us to finish strong.

However, an important distinction needs to be made here. Though living in God's yes is not meant to run us ragged, it will cost us our lives. Jesus invites us—sometimes in baby steps, and sometimes through significant experiences—to lay down our lives, to die to our flesh, and to entrust ourselves to Him when, from all natural appearances, it'll seem like the enemy is winning.

But the great news is, *we* win in the end. And anytime we die to ourselves, we find ourselves more fully in Him, living more boldly for Him. Nothing can separate us from His love, and He will see to it that we get safely home. Life in God's yes is the only life for those of us who are in Christ Jesus.

Then comes the deeper matter of our no. As we begin to grasp the authority we possess in Christ, we learn to draw a line in the sand and limit the work the enemy is allowed to do in our lives and in our world today.

Do you realize how profoundly God has empowered us for this journey? Jesus told us that He has given us authority over all of the power of the enemy. When it comes to God's promises, He says yes to us so we can stand in battle and say no to the enemy of our souls.

Read this life-changing verse: "I have given you authority to trample on snakes and scorpions and to overcome all the power of the enemy; nothing will harm you" (Luke 10:19).

Jesus may have given us the authority, but we have to *take* it. This is our time. This is our day. Will we have the unction to say no to un-appointed tasks? Will we have the courage to become prayer warriors who stand in the gap for the needs of our day? Will we look at the injustices and the evil all around us, stomp our foot, and say, "Not on my watch"?

Will we learn to use our no in a way that sends the enemy reeling? We have the authority to stand in the gap for our children, our marriages, our communities, and our fellow believers who serve all across the earth today. When we pray for the poor, the human trafficking victim, and the orphan, things *will* change on the earth.

Read this powerful passage from Eugene Peterson's *Message* paraphrase of Ephesians 6:10–18:

> And that about wraps it up. God is strong, and he wants you strong. So take everything the Master has set out for you, well-made weapons of the best materials. And put them to use so you will be able to stand up to everything the Devil throws your way.

This is no afternoon athletic contest that we'll walk away from and forget about in a couple of hours. This is for keeps, a life-or-death fight to the finish against the Devil and all his angels.

Be prepared. You're up against far more than you can handle on your own. Take all the help you can get, every weapon God has issued, so that when it's all over but the shouting you'll still be on your feet. Truth, righteousness, peace, faith, and salvation are more than words. Learn how to apply them. You'll need them throughout your life.

God's Word is an indispensable weapon. In the same way, prayer is essential in this ongoing warfare. Pray hard and long. Pray for your brothers and sisters. Keep your eyes open. Keep each other's spirits up so that no one falls behind or drops out.

Will you dare to give Him your yes on a daily basis? Will you embrace the gritty faith required to walk in the influence assigned to you and to enforce the victory that Jesus has already won for you? In his book *You Were Born for This*, Bruce Wilkinson reminds us that God invites us to partner with heaven so that miracles can happen on earth. He makes these important points:

- God is constantly at work in supernatural ways in our world, and He has much He wants to get done.
- God is actively looking for loyal partners—people who consistently care about what He cares about.
- God is regularly nudging people to respond, but most people miss His intentions or simply say no.[2]

What would it look like in your life if you started saying yes?

God gives us everything we need to live powerful, fruitful, godly lives. He gives us His promises so that we can lay hold of them and participate in the kingdom story He's writing on the earth today. He's issued you a loving, clear invitation, one that calls for your permission, your submission, your obedience, and your faith. Will you say yes?

The Power of God's Spirit Within Us

We are in a spiritual battle. Today. Right now.

Jesus will one day return—sooner than later, I believe—for us, His bride, the church. The only reason we're alive, the only reason we're living and breathing at this moment, is to get ready for His return.

Our enemy, the devil, camps on the assumption that if he baits us into busyness, we'll forget about our adoption as daughters and sons. And sadly, he gets away with this scheme far too often.

But not with us. Not anymore.

We have the power of the risen Lord alive and at work within us. We've been given authority over the enemy. We walk in God's presence as we live here on earth. When we pray in faith, mountains move. When we say to that enemy, "No more!" he *has* to obey us.

On the other hand, when we forget who we are, it's like we drop our shield and fling aside our authority. The enemy sees the opportunity and attempts to occupy land that belongs to us. Yet Scripture tells us that God has *not* given us a spirit of fear, but He *has* given us a spirit of power, love, and a sound mind. Read the Amplified version of this great passage:

> For God did not give us a spirit of timidity (of cowardice, of craven and cringing and fawning fear), but [He has given us a spirit] of power and of love and of calm and well-balanced mind and discipline and self-control.
>
> 2 Timothy 1:7 AMP

For us to accomplish God's purposes on the earth in our lifetime and to stand in the last days, we need a deeper understanding of this passage and what it means for us. Each one of us battles moments of fear, intimidation, and smallness. And if we say we don't, we're either lying or we think too highly of ourselves.

On our own, we're no match for the enemy. And on our strongest day, a gust of wind could still knock us off our feet. We're wise to know when we're outmatched, because it compels us to trust in the strength of our God. It's impossible for Him to fail us.

On our own, we are truly vulnerable sheep. But even so, the lack of courage that makes us want to run and hide is not from God. He's given us—dependent, vulnerable sheep—a different kind of spirit. One of

- Power
- Love
- Self-control

Jesus reminds us that we're sheep so we'll remember that we're dependent. And to the extent that we depend on God will we walk in His power and rest in His care. Let's take a deeper look at the Spirit that God has put inside of us:

Power: *dunamis* = *explosive power*

We cannot fathom the power made available to us because of Christ in us! Scripture says that the same power that raised Christ from the dead is alive in us. Read this powerful truth that belongs to us:

> I pray that your hearts will be flooded with light so that you can understand the confident hope he has given to those he called— his holy people who are his rich and glorious inheritance.
>
> I also pray that you will understand the incredible greatness of God's power for us who believe him. This is the same mighty power that raised Christ from the dead and seated him in the place of honor at God's right hand in the heavenly realms.
>
> Ephesians 1:18–20 NLT

If the power that raised Christ from the dead is at work in us right now, how different should our lives be from those with no Spirit-life in their souls?

Jesus has not given us a spirit that compels us to cringe in the corner because we're intimidated. He has given us a spirit of power. Thayer's Greek–English lexicon unpacks the word *power* in this verse this way (think about how these words apply to your life, your circumstances, and the spirit with which God has equipped you to navigate through life):

1. Strength power, ability
2. Inherent power, power residing in a thing by virtue of its nature, or which a person or thing exerts and puts forth
3. Power for performing miracles
4. Moral power and excellence of soul
5. The power and influence which belong to riches and wealth
6. Power and resources arising from numbers
7. Power consisting in or resting upon armies, forces, hosts[3]

Just because we don't *feel* the power that God has placed within us, doesn't mean it's not there. Familiarize yourself with this truth and remind yourself daily that God has given you a spirit of dynamic power—moral, influential power, an excellence of soul, and a supernatural ability to accomplish your tasks, face your fears, climb your mountains, and stand in battle. You have what you need to be mighty in the land God has assigned to you.

Love: *agape = affection, goodwill, charity, love*

Dr. Wiersbe unpacks this part of the passage insightfully:

> The Holy Spirit also gives us love. If we have love for lost souls and for the people of God, we will be able to endure suffering

and accomplish the work of God. Selfishness leads to fear because, if we are selfish, we are interested only in what we will get out of serving God, and we will be afraid of losing prestige, power, or money. True Christian love, energized by the Spirit (Rom. 5:5), enables us to sacrifice for others and not be afraid. The Spirit gives us love (Gal. 5:22).[4]

Just as we're no match for our enemy on our own, we are simply unable to love others the way Christ loves them without His Spirit at work in us. We all tend toward selfishness and self-preservation, but that tendency is not from God. He's put a life-giving, beautifully radical, self-sacrificing spirit in us that makes us come alive when we love others the way He has loved us.

When you notice your tendency to think only of yourself, don't condemn yourself, because there's NO condemnation for those of us who are in Christ Jesus. But do rise up, stretch out your arms, worship God, and ask for an awakening of His heart within you. He loves to answer prayers like these! Then, by sheer obedience, get up and go out and love someone.

Pay for someone's coffee. Buy grocery gift cards and hand them out to the homeless people in your city. Send money to an organization that feeds the poor. Volunteer at church. Be tenacious and ask God to grow your heart of compassion for those He loves. Look for opportunities to share your faith story.

When we walk in the love that Christ has put in us, our capacity for that love grows by leaps and bounds. It's like we activate a spiritual muscle, one that begs to be engaged. When we love others in a way that goes beyond our own natural instincts, we tend to the deepest desire of God's heart for the world—that the world may know His love. And as we deeply love others, something in our own soul gets healed along the way.

Dear friends, since God so loved us, we also ought to love one another. No one has ever seen God; but if we love one another, God lives in us and his love is made complete in us. This is how we know that we live in him and he in us: He has given us of his Spirit. . . . In this world we are like Jesus. There is no fear in love. But perfect love drives out fear, because fear has to do with punishment. The one who fears is not made perfect in love.

1 John 4:11–13, 17–18

Sound Mind, Self-Control: *sophronismos = sound mind, moderation, self-control*[5]

Years ago my thought-life seemed to have a mind of its own. (Pun intended.) I honestly believed I had little to no control over my rogue thoughts. Anxiety and fear seemed my constant companions. I feared for my safety in unknown settings. I worried that my troubles were a taste of something worse waiting just around the corner for me. I cared far too much about what others thought of me.

Then one day, when I'd grown sick and tired of being tossed around by my anxious heart, I sensed God's invitation to put some boundaries around my thought-life. That's when everything changed for me. I share that story in my book *The Uncommon Woman*. Here's a taste of what God did for me:

Something amazing started to happen. Peace and security filled in the gaps of my life where turmoil and insecurity used to be. By refusing to entertain even a single thought about what others might be thinking of me, and instead filling my mind with the wonder of God's love, everything in me and around me changed. Each day I took a step in the right direction. Eventually I tiptoed onto the edges of my promised land. I felt freedom's grass between my toes; I breathed in the pure air of unpolluted acceptance; I ran though my very own fields of grace, and I determined that I would never again return to my captivity.[6]

174

A sound mind is a gift from God.

Just a caveat here: To those who struggle with mental health issues and chemical imbalances, I say to you, *May the Lord Himself wrap you up in His grace and heal you through and through! And in the meantime, may He surround you with people who love you right where you are, and who will offer you grace as you wrestle with a very real battle.*

The passage from 2 Timothy 1:7 is sometimes misused in a way that shames those with mental health issues and suggests that if they had more faith, they wouldn't struggle like they do. We have to be so careful with our faith-talk when it comes to the battles others face daily.

Whenever I address the issue of mental health on my radio show, the phones light up. We cannot fathom the number of families impacted by mental illness. My heart breaks when I hear stories of how we—as God's people—have responded to those with this particular struggle. It's downright painful. *Lord, help us to offer grace, to walk in love, and to be to them as You have been to us.*

That said, when Scripture says that God has put His Spirit in us, and one of the benefits of His presence in our lives is a sound mind, what does that mean exactly? Here's a list from my study Bible:

- Safe thinking
- Good judgment
- Disciplined thought patterns
- The ability to understand and make right decisions
- Self-control[7]

Who *doesn't* want to walk in power, abound in love, and embrace a sound mind and thought process from a biblical perspective?

I know I do. This is why I pray daily, out loud for my own ears to hear: *Lord, may I abound in love, more and more. May I increase daily in all wisdom, knowledge, and depth of insight. May I understand the times and know what to do. May I highly discern Your wisdom, Your ways, and Your truth. May I walk purely and blamelessly before You so that my life will honor You in life and death, and so that I will bear the fruit of righteousness.*

Craft a prayer of your own and lay claim to the power, the love, and the sound mind God has made available to you. Pray for and give grace to those who struggle. But grab hold of God's promises for yourself and renew your mind with them. He's given you the power to do so.

Power to Stop Evil

Once we wrap our minds and hearts around the idea that God hasn't given us a spirit of fear, but one of power, love, and a sound mind, we can better understand our role on the earth today. Read this passage from 2 Thessalonians 2:7–8:

> For the secret power of lawlessness is already at work; but the one who now holds it back will continue to do so till he is taken out of the way. And then the lawless one will be revealed, whom the Lord Jesus will overthrow with the breath of his mouth and destroy by the splendor of his coming.

Even though it seems that evil runs rampant all around us, there's actually a force that holds the enemy back, a power that keeps him from utterly destroying everything around us. The devil has to deal with a restraint that allows him only partial influence for the time being. So what *is* that restraint, exactly?

Some scholars differ on their interpretation of who or what the restrainer is, but the most consistent thought among biblical scholars is that the restrainer is the power of the Holy Spirit at work within the lives of believers. This interpretation makes the most sense when you consider that the primary way God works on the earth is through His people.

Think about that for a moment. Certain schemes of the enemy come to nothing because of your presence on the earth today. You have angels who guard and guide, and the mighty power of the Holy Spirit within you. Power surrounds you, even when you're unaware. Though terrible things do happen to God's people during our time on the earth, many more evils are avoided because of our presence here.

And think about your prayers for a moment. When you pray protection around your children or your marriage or your city, imagine what evil scheme came to nothing because of *your* prayers. You are a part of the resistance army!

Now imagine the rapture. And even if you don't believe the rapture will take place prior to the tribulation, do this: Try to picture a world without Christians—people who love and serve and pray and give. Imagine a world absent of those who deeply grieve over the sins of the world and who pray with conviction and passion. Picture a world without the multitude of Christians who love and serve the poor and give generously to feed them. Imagine this planet without the heroes who valiantly rescue young girls from human trafficking. Without the Spirit-led men and women who go to war-torn areas and bandage wounds, hold babies, and pray for the sick.

Picture a world without godly families who take in the neighbor kid who comes from a broken home. Picture the churches empty, with no vacation Bible school, no worship services on Wednesdays or Sundays. No more missionaries, youth pastors, or children's ministers. No more Christian authors, speakers, or radio hosts. No more Christian athletes, business owners, or teachers. All gone. Vanished from the earth. Wickedness running rampant and freely in every city. What will the world be like?

Important side note: This is not to say that *only* Christians are kind, or that Christians are *always* and *only* kind. We've all acted in ways that fall far beneath our spiritual privilege. And there are plenty of unbelievers who've stepped up to help and give in ways that should make us blush. That part of their nature reflects the image of their Creator. But it's the Spirit of the living God in us that turns our actions into offerings that not only multiply on earth, but also echo into eternity.

For the unbeliever, a kind act—as kind as it is—is weighed down by the gravity of a fallen world. Good deeds are good deeds. But actions prompted by faith ignite a change in the spiritual atmosphere, and that's where the real battles are won and lost (see Ephesians 6:12). It's the difference between a boy who gives his lunch to just anybody and a boy who gives his lunch to Jesus (see John 6:9–13).

Even so, consider the millions of Christians today who walk the earth, who follow the lead of the Holy Spirit within them, who pray for God's purposes, and who stand against the enemy's schemes on the earth. Try to picture all of the spiritual activity in the heavenly realm that takes place because of the way we stand in faith on the earth.

Now imagine all of this spiritual activity coming to a sudden stop. Believers are gone from the earth. The wall of resistance we provide suddenly lifts. Wickedness floods in without any opposition. Imagine.

Read what pastor and author Jeff Kinley has to say about the force that currently holds back the enemy:

> Meanwhile, godlessness continues seeping through the dam of decency, building in volume and intensity. Eventually that dam will burst, and the last wall of virtue will be breached. I believe the rapture of the church is the event that will set

in motion this final deluge of ungodliness. . . . I believe this restrainer is the Holy Spirit. Granted, a large portion of His work in the world happens through believers because the Holy Spirit indwells all Christians. His presence and power in the church does much of Christ's work here on earth. It is He who currently holds back lawlessness, hindering the global advance of sin until the final days. And He's using us in that process! However, because we're living this in real time, it can be difficult to see what a difference Christians make just by *being here*.[8]

I once heard a man say something to this effect: *Some Christians live such spiritually irrelevant lives that the enemy makes no plans to oppose them.* Ouch. But isn't it true? Scripture is clear that some who are saved will have nothing to show for it. They'll have lived such earthbound lives that they'll have not even a single gem to place at Jesus' feet (see 1 Corinthians 3:9–15). Painfully difficult to comprehend, isn't it? What a waste to live only for ourselves!

When you consider believers who fight very few battles because they live mostly for themselves, we have to ask ourselves: Is it really the worst thing to be harassed by the enemy because we walk intimately with God and engage with His purposes on the earth? We may get pushed around a bit, but *we* are on the winning side.

Nothing—absolutely nothing—can separate us from the love of our precious Savior. And our light and momentary troubles are achieving something profoundly beautiful in our life that strengthens and beautifies us now, and changes how we'll live in eternity.

For our light and momentary troubles are achieving for us an eternal glory that far outweighs them all.

2 Corinthians 4:17

Can you see how important it is to believe the beautiful, powerful truth about our worth, our value, our position in Christ, and our call upon the earth today?

If we stand in the truth of who we are because of Christ Jesus, we can stand powerfully in this day and make a difference in our world.

We can pray with authority and know that God hears our prayers—and sends angels into action on our behalf *because of* our request. We can walk humbly in the world because we know God has our backs. We can love others as Christ has loved us because He has so lavished His love upon us.

We have nothing to prove and all of eternity to live for. Oh, the love of Jesus. May we stand courageously, pray tenaciously, and love audaciously. May we give our whole lives as an offering to Him! May we wholeheartedly embrace this reality: We are heirs of God, full of the power of the Holy Spirit, and called to serve Him courageously for such a time as this.

The ground under your feet, the season of life you're in, the battles you face, the dreams in your heart . . . it's *holy ground*. And God is with you. As you walk forward with a heart of faith, remember this: You are full of the power of the Holy Spirit, you abound in the love of God, and you are rich with the wisdom and clarity that Jesus provides. So from this day forward, may your yes and no reflect the fact that all of heaven is on your side.

Spirit of the living God, fall afresh on me!
Put me right where I'm thinking wrong. Fan the flame within me, Lord! Release in me a fresh revelation of Your power and Your love. Open my eyes to see You at work everywhere I go. Awaken me to the overwhelming wonder of Your grace and mercy for everyone I meet. Teach me more about the authority I have in You. Help me to walk

and talk and pray with boldness and courage, authority and strength, humility and hope. Forgive me for the land I've handed over to the enemy because of my own unbelief. Help me to reclaim what the enemy has stolen from me. Help me to stand in the gap for those who cannot defend themselves. Help me to reject any notion of inferiority and insecurity. They're NOT from You, so they don't belong in me! Fill me once again with the knowledge of Your will. May Your peace be my guide so that every step I take and every commitment I make is prompted by Your direction in my life. I am Yours and You are mine. Thank You, Lord, for making me an heir. Help me to live up to my high privilege and calling. In Jesus' name, I pray. Amen.

Personal Reflection

1. When you consider that God has entrusted you with a measure of delegated authority and influence, what thoughts come to mind?

2. Think about a time, event, or moment when you had a strong sense of God's power at work in and through you. What was different about that moment from other moments?

3. In what ways do you long to grow in your spiritual influence (e.g., praying in the power of the Holy Spirit, serving the poor, strengthening the church)? Do you sense God's invitation to upgrade your faith? To believe Him more firmly in certain areas?

4. When does unbelief most plague you (e.g., when you blow it, when you're in conflict, when you're sleep deprived)?

5. In what ways can you strengthen your stance so that when the winds of unbelief blow, you remain strong in your sense of who you are and of who God is *in* you in spite

of your own weaknesses (e.g., memorize Scripture, call a godly friend, pray out loud)?

A *Wise Word*

There is no doubt that we are living in some of the most challenging days the world has ever seen. But you can face these times victoriously because God has given you a sound mind; He has given you the promises of His Word; and He has given you the leadership of His Spirit. Never has there been a more crucial time for you to operate in faith and not fear and to believe for a mighty move of God to take place on this earth![9]

Group Discussion Starters

1. Who do you know who seems to walk with a sense of humble-yet-bold God-given authority? What about that person most impacts you?

2. When you consider that God has assigned to you delegated authority and influence, what thoughts come to your mind?

3. If you could stand in power against an evil in our day, what would it be?

4. Do you sense an invitation from God to engage more fully with Him in some way (through prayer, financial giving, serving, etc.)?

5. Theoretically, what's the difference between a Christian (or a church) that is mostly talk and a Christian (or a church) that functions with power? Without identifying specific people or churches, make the distinction between *all talk* and *talk with power*.

Faith Declaration

I declare in the mighty name of Jesus that I am an anointed, appointed child of God! I am filled with the Holy Spirit and empowered by His love. I walk in the Lord's presence as I live here on earth. I have eyes to see, ears to hear, and a heart to do His will. I refuse to throw my yes around like it doesn't matter. Life is a gift, and my time is a gift. God invites me to walk with Him and do the next thing He gives me to do. I am loved, called, and fully equipped to live the powerful life God has assigned to me. I refuse the rat race because God has called me to the sacred race. And I will run with holy passion and conviction. In Jesus' name I pray, Amen!

✦ 12 ✦

Closing Thoughts

Say Yes to a Life That Counts

We consider and look not to the things that are
seen but to the things that are unseen; for the things
that are visible are temporal (brief and fleeting),
but the things that are invisible are deathless and
everlasting.

2 Corinthians 4:18 AMP

This is the life of spiritual balance: a life that centers
on and draws from heaven's love. This love is never
stagnant. It is always growing, always refining and
always dealing with sin and healing pain. It is always
flowing in, making a difference, and then flowing
out to a lost and dying world. Take Him in, make
Him your focus, and see what love will do.[1]

I miss my dad. He was both snarky and kind, a loving grandpa,
and sometimes a grouchy ol' thing. He made us laugh,

challenged us to think, and never sugarcoated his words. With strong leadership, he guided our family—seven kids, all of us married, nineteen grandchildren, and two great-grandchildren. We all knew how much he loved us. He would have given his life for his family.

My dad went to be with Jesus a few years ago.

I'll never forget the last few hours of his time here on earth. Wracked with pain, he wrestled between restless discomfort and total unresponsiveness. He chose hospice care at home. Wrapped in a blanket, slouched in his favorite chair in the living room, my mom and brothers and sisters and I surrounded him. We felt overwhelmed and sad, and we so wished we could do more to make him comfortable. The pain that wracked his body broke our hearts. The room felt oppressive and thick with despair.

My mom left his side and walked into the kitchen. She buried her face in her hands and wept. My sisters and I got up and went over to her. Her chest heaved as she hyperventilated. She couldn't steady herself. The man she'd loved and lived with for almost sixty years was about to leave this earth. Inconsolable, she wrapped her arms around us and cried, "I'm having a hard time breathing. My heart is breaking! And I think my blood pressure is way up right now. I need you to pray for me. And for your dad!"

Suddenly Luke 10:19 came to mind: "I have given you authority to trample on snakes and scorpions and to overcome all the power of the enemy; nothing will harm you."

My sisters and I pulled our mom close and invited Jesus into the center of our heartbreak. We took authority over the anxiety that threatened to swallow our mom alive. We prayed for her heart, for her blood pressure, and for her whole soul to know the peace of God. Then we looked over at our dad, and with the authority of Christ in us, we spoke to the pain that raged inside of him. We asked God to calm the storm, to give our dad peace, and to usher him safely from this life to the next.

After that prayer, everything changed.

My mom's blood pressure settled down. My dad's countenance softened. And the room filled with peace. My brother Jeff opened his Bible and read the Twenty-third Psalm.

We were on holy ground.

My brother Greg pulled out his guitar and sang one of my dad's favorites songs, "The Old Rugged Cross." We harmonized softly, with passion. Tears streamed down our faces. My sister Karen scooted up close to my dad's good ear and sang a beautiful song to him titled "Welcome Home." Then she pulled out a love letter my mom had written to my dad for his eightieth birthday. Her voice broke as she reminded my dad how much she loved him.

Heaven was near. We could feel it in our skin.

My mom traded places with Karen and nestled close to my dad. She put her wrinkled hands on his face. Through her tears she declared her love for our papa. She said, "Ed, you are, and will always be, the love of my life. I love you, honey. Thank you for all the wonderful years together. You've been a fighter for so long. You've fought a good fight. It's okay to rest now and go home with Jesus."

Our sobs filled the room.

Dad was totally unresponsive at this time.

The dark room, which had felt oppressive only minutes before, emanated unfathomable peace. We surrounded Dad and silently prayed for him. We embraced our last moments with him.

Suddenly, his eyes opened wide. He looked up to the corner of the room near the ceiling and smiled, like he saw something familiar or comforting. Then he locked his gaze on my mom.

He reached out his arms for her and pulled her face to his. He took a few more breaths . . . then he went home with Jesus. *"Precious in the sight of the Lord is the death of his faithful servants" (Psalm 116:15).*

My dad finished his race. He loved us. He loved Jesus. Oh, how I miss him.

Life is sacred.

And death is sacred.

May we all live well so we can finish well.

None of us knows how many days God has assigned to us on this earth. But we have today. We have God's presence and His promises. And we're called to think long, to think past this life, to live with eternity in mind.

We have today. We don't know about tomorrow. So this moment? This gift from God? May we open our hands and offer it back to Jesus. May we live, move, and find our life completely and profoundly in Him.

You and Me

I pray that you've sensed God's very personal presence with you on this journey. If you and I could share a cup of coffee or tea together, I'd share these final thoughts with you:

You are far more loved than you can comprehend. God is nearer than you think and far more interested and invested in your journey than you can even imagine.

Your prayers *do* initiate change in the atmosphere. So pray. With precision, passion, and power.

There is now, because of Christ Jesus, NO condemnation—ever, at all, or ever will be—for you because *you're in Him.* You're free to be a work in progress from this day forward until Jesus receives you in heaven, when He shows you the beautiful place He's prepared for you. What a day that will be!

In the days to come you'll be tempted to dawdle with things that don't matter, things that are beneath your spiritual privilege. All things are lawful, but they're not all profitable; all things are lawful, but not everything edifies and makes us stronger. In fact, some of our freedoms can potentially weaken us (see 1 Corinthians 10:23).

I pray you'll care about your influence enough to be ruthless with any destructive and indulgent tendencies.

There'll be certain days when your current circumstances stir up old hurts. Don't overreact or even overstate how you're feeling. Keep your eyes on Christ and your heart of faith engaged. Trust that when God allows old stuff to surface, it's because He intends to set the plow a little deeper in your soul so He can heal you on a deeper level.

God heals us deeply so we can love more fully. And oftentimes His healing work comes just before a breakthrough. Trust Him to heal your soul, make you whole, and lead you to your next place of promise.

During particular busy seasons of life, it's tempting to let go of the important things that strengthen and nourish us. Whenever you need to, go back to chapter 10 and review the sacred steps and reengage in the ways that God tells you to.

Ask God to do the impossible in and through you. Dare to stretch your arms open wide and ask for a fresh filling of the Holy Spirit—every single day. Do the next thing He tells you to do. Persevere in hard times. Stay in the Word as your lifeline and plumb line. Trust God to make a way where there is no way. And keep humility and courage as your constant travel companions.

You'll have days when you'll feel completely overwhelmed and at a loss. You'll feel sure you followed Jesus to this place, but you'll wonder why you don't sense His grace. Oftentimes, it's not that we're overworked, we're just *under*rested. Rest is the most neglected discipline among Christians—ironic, when you consider we're invited to dwell and rest in the shadow of the Lord's wing (see Psalm 91:1)!

When you find yourself utterly exhausted, again, refuse the condemnation, but do make room for rest, replenishment, and even for times of enjoyment and renewal. It's prideful *not* to rest. And it makes for a miserable journey. Remember, rest is both God's gift to us and a forward-moving discipline that's critical to our journey.

Sometimes you'll find yourself wrapped up in the urgency of the moment and you'll forget about your place in the bigger kingdom story. Tuck a reminder in your Bible or on your fridge to pray for your persecuted brothers and sisters around the world. Jesus specifically asked us to pray for them.

We've got fellow Christ-followers around the world who suffer for the sake of the gospel in ways we cannot fathom. We cannot and must not leave them uncovered. Pray for their protection and provision, for boldness and courage, and for favor with their oppressors that many might trust Jesus because of their heroic sacrifice.

Can we pause here for a minute?

I admit that I'm about to step on a few toes here. But by now, I pray I've earned your trust and you'll allow me to talk about an issue that impacts each and every one of us. Here it is: *giving.*

We cannot talk about our *sacred yes* without addressing the issue of finances as it relates to our faith. Here's a fact: Our offerings—both great and small—impact the world and change us in the process. Jesus talked about money and stewardship more than anything else. Maybe it's because He knew we'd tend to compartmentalize our faith.

And so, I invite you to grow in the grace of giving. I promise you (better yet, Scripture promises you), when you become a *flow through* account of God's blessings, it will radically change your life.

Did you know that over 90 percent of Christians don't tithe? Imagine that! Churches and ministries struggle daily to function on a fraction of the income that they should have from God's people.

But don't hear this from me as an ought-to or should-do.

We've learned—beyond our wildest imagination—that giving is a *get-to*. And just to be clear: We don't give to get. We don't give to manipulate God. He can't be manipulated. This isn't at all about some kind of name-it-and-claim-it theology.

However, I'm convinced with all my heart that we will not fully mature, nor will we reach the fullness of our faith, until our faith has impacted our finances.

If you don't have the faith or the means to give 10 percent, start small and be consistent. Ask God to grant you a gift of faith with regard to giving. But get a vision beyond your 10 percent. Picture yourself growing in your ability to give and tend to the needs around you. When you step up, God will release fresh favor over your life. That's His promise. Plus, we activate a spiritual muscle when we give, and it gets stronger the more we use it.

As Christians, we don't live by the world's economy of buying and selling. We live by the kingdom principle of sowing and reaping. God's economy is not in trouble. It's as strong as it's always been. God has an endless supply of storehouses that—I'm convinced—sit untapped because we're too afraid to live by faith. When we send our treasures on ahead, they're protected from any market crash on earth. Jesus had a lot to say about our treasures:

> Some people store up treasures *in their homes* here on earth. *This is a shortsighted practice*—don't undertake it. Moths and rust will eat up any treasure you may store here. Thieves may break into *your homes* and steal *your precious trinkets.* Instead, put up your treasures in heaven where moths do not attack,

where rust does not corrode, and where thieves are barred at the door. For where your treasure is, there your heart will be also.

Matthew 6:19–21 THE VOICE

I believe that the majority of Christians don't tithe or give generously because of fear. But when has fear ever been a suitable motivator for the believer? We live by faith! If there ever was a time when the world needs to hear and see the influence of the church and of Christian ministries, it's *now*. This isn't a time to pull back in fear. It's a time to step up in faith and be counted. This can and should be the church's finest hour!

For years I've prayed that we will one day see a revival of the tithe in the church. Imagine the influence in our world if churches and ministries were suddenly abundantly funded! What if we were personally and excitedly motivated to be involved in the greater story God is writing on the earth today? And what if—instead of 5 or 7 percent of believers—we saw 90 percent of believers fully engaged in giving as a lifestyle? Do you know how many more miracle stories of provision we'd all have to share? God comes through for the giver in ways the hoarder will never experience.

I care so very much about the church and about Christian ministries, and I want them to thrive for the sake of the kingdom, and I care deeply about you too. I absolutely do not want you to miss out on seeing the goodness of God as you seek first His kingdom (see Matthew 6:33).

Don't give grudgingly or hastily. Give joyfully. And do know this: God has a bigger shovel. He won't be outdone. You give, and He will pour back blessings into your life in ways too many to count. I promise you—better yet, God promises you—that if you engage your faith in your finances, you'll be in for an adventure that will rock your world.

I didn't intend to end this book, or my time with you, with a message on giving, but it suddenly feels very important that I do so.

For the world's sake, for the kingdom's sake, and for your own influence's sake, become a faith-filled, spirit-filled, audacious giver—and not just financially, but in every other way as well.

Remember too—not just in our giving, but in every other area of life—that healthy boundaries and sacred disciplines can quickly become self-serving unless we see them as a framework for God to keep us strong and steady and dependent on Him so He can do the impossible in and through us.

In fact, I'll leave you with a passage that my husband, Kevin, and I have prayed for years. We want to abound in every good work. We want to be generous in all that we do. In every way possible. We want to help as many people as we can while we have breath in our lungs. So we pray this passage (and I believe it's for you too):

> But I will say this *to encourage your generosity*: the one who plants little harvests little, and the one who plants plenty harvests plenty. Giving grows out of the heart—otherwise, you've reluctantly grumbled "yes" because you felt you had to or because you couldn't say "no," *but this isn't the way God wants it.* For *we know that* "God loves a cheerful giver." God is ready to overwhelm you with more blessings than you could ever imagine so that you'll always be taken care of in every way and you'll have more than enough to share. Remember what is written *about the One who trusts in the Lord*:
> He scattered abroad; He gave *freely* to the poor; His righteousness endures throughout the ages.
> The same One who has put seed into the hands of the sower and brought bread to fill our stomachs will provide and multiply the resources you invest and produce an abundant harvest from your righteous actions. You will be made rich in everything so

that your generosity *will spill over in every direction. Through us* your generosity is at work inspiring praise and thanksgiving to God. For this mission will do more than bring food and water to fellow believers in need—it will overflow in a cascade of *praises and* thanksgivings for our God. . . . Praise God for this *incredible, unbelievable,* indescribable gift!

2 Corinthians 9:6–12, 15 THE VOICE

May you live such a radical, faith-filled life, sowing seeds wherever you go, expecting that God will move on every act prompted by your faith, because *you* are a kingdom-builder!

Imagine the end of your life.

Picture the multitudes celebrating your presence on this earth. They rise up and praise God because of how *your* life impacted theirs.

All of your sowing and reaping, your praying and believing, your trusting and obeying has created a harvest of life all around you. You gave Jesus your yes and He multiplied it in ways you could never have imagined.

Picture Jesus with that smile that reaches His eyes, ready to greet you. He stretches His arms open wide and wraps you up in a hug. With His precious nail-scarred hands He holds your shoulders, looks into your eyes, and says, "Thank you, My child. Well done. You did it. You've been so faithful with all I entrusted to you.

"Now, come and see what *I've* been up to."

Precious Lord,

With my arms open wide and my heart set on You, I ask, dear Lord, fill me anew with the power and presence of Your Holy Spirit! Fill me up and pour me out! Give me bold, audacious faith that I might dare to ask You for the impossible! Awaken my heart toward the things

You care about so that Your kingdom becomes my highest concern. Fan the flame of generosity within me that I may give away record amounts in this coming year. I want to participate in Your kingdom story with every aspect of my life. I am called, loved, chosen, equipped, and empowered to live a life far beyond my own abilities. I have access to all of the riches of heaven, so I boldly lay hold of them for Your name's sake, O Lord. Give me eyes to see, ears to hear, and a heart to do Your will. Lift the grace for every lesser thing in my life. Help me lose my taste for the things that weaken me and diminish my influence. May Your Word come alive to me like it never has before! May I rightly handle Your Word, preach it with boldness, and believe it with every ounce of faith You give me. Awaken me to a whole new level of generous giving and generous living. I want to see miracles in my life and in this world. Here I am, Lord. In me and through me, glorify Your name. Amen.

A Wise Word

Notice *you* are in charge of holding your mind at attention. Each and every day you have the power to choose whether to be attentive and focused or dull and distracted. . . . Allow the weight of God's Word and the tempering and training of the Holy Spirit to quicken and develop the weak or injured areas of your life. *Shift your focus from how you look in your clothing to who you are in your spirit.* Above all, *do not fear your strength.* . . . Remember, when all the earth is filled with fear and is wondering what is going on, the God of heaven and earth, the Creator of all, calls you to display his fearsome wonder in how you portray your life.[2]

Therefore, my beloved brethren, be firm (steadfast), immovable, always abounding in the work of the Lord [always being superior, excelling, doing more than enough in the service of the Lord], knowing and being continually aware that your labor in the Lord is not futile [it is never wasted or to no purpose].

1 Corinthians 15:58 AMP

Wow. What an honor it's been to make this journey with you! May you continue to walk in the Lord's presence as you live here on earth (Psalm 116:9). And may you live and breathe and serve and give for an audience of One.

Until we meet again.

Susie Larson

✤ 13 ✤

Bonus Chapter
Faith and Fitness Challenge

We run for the crown that we will wear for eternity. So I don't run aimlessly. *I don't let my eyes drift off the finish line.* When I box, I don't throw punches in the air. I discipline my body and make it my slave so that after *all this,* after I have brought the gospel to others, I will still be qualified *to win the prize.*

1 Corinthians 9:25–27 THE VOICE

He has chosen you. He has His heart set on you. And as you draw near to Him, He'll draw near to you. Instead of striving and hoping you'll be enough for Him, put your hope in His unfailing love, knowing it'll be more than enough for you.[1]

On my radio show *Live the Promise,* we invited our listeners to participate in a six-week faith and fitness challenge. Year one, we had approximately four hundred people sign up. Year two, we had close to four thousand join us! Over and over again I heard from listeners who loved this challenge because, for the most part, these disciplines didn't require extra time, but rather a different focus.

Will you join us?

You'll notice that the disciplines each week are easy to do— but just as easy not to. Lean in. Engage with God as we take this journey. *You* carry the treasure of the Spirit of the living God in you! Throughout the next six weeks, ponder the power of God's cleansing work in your life. He's made you new! No spot or stain on you! Care for your physical and spiritual health in a way that honors God.

Each week you'll add a new daily physical and spiritual discipline. Then, with each week that follows, you keep your previous disciplines and add the new ones assigned for that week. Are you ready? Here we go!

Week 1

This Week's Disciplines

- *Drink Water*
- *Read the Word*

We receive many health benefits when we drink plenty of water. And even more important, God changes us from the inside out when we read His Word, believe what He says, and follow His lead. This week we'll focus on the cleansing aspects of drinking plenty of water and of spending time in God's Word.

Physical Discipline: Drink Water

Experts suggest we need eight to ten glasses of water a day. My husband added this one discipline to his daily routine and lost ten pounds in one month! My friend and fitness expert Wendie Pett suggests we drink the equivalent to half our body weight (in ounces). So if you weigh two hundred pounds, you need about one hundred ounces of water a day.

Either way, it's time to up your water intake, and here's why:

- Great for hair and skin
- Helps digestion and metabolism
- Helps muscle function

Dangers of Dehydration

- Muscle spasms and cramps
- Neurological impairment
- Digestive issues
- Dry skin and hair
- Headaches
- Water retention

When we drink too much soda, we lose our taste for water. I challenge you to find a fun water bottle and raise your water intake starting today!

Spiritual Discipline: Read the Word

If you don't have a regularly established quiet time, take that first step. Set aside ten to fifteen minutes each day to open the Word and prayerfully read. If you're new to reading the Bible, start with the books of Psalms, Proverbs, or the gospel of John. If you already have an established quiet time, the challenge to you is to extend your time by adding a few extra minutes each day dedicated solely to reading God's Word. Scripture is living and active and will change your life!

Here's why God's Word is so important to us:

- It's living and active and brings life, strength, and direction to our soul.
- It offers us wisdom and reveals God's heart.
- It teaches us how to live and brings clarity where there's confusion.

Everyone who drinks this water will be thirsty again, but whoever drinks the water I give them will never thirst. Indeed, the water I give them will become in them a spring of water welling up to eternal life.

John 4:13–14

Jesus answered, "It is written: 'Man shall not live on bread alone, but on every word that comes from the mouth of God.'"

Matthew 4:4

Jesus, I pause today and remember that You came to earth for me. Thank You for living, for dying, and for defeating sin and death on the cross. I commit this journey to You. Increase my capacity to know You, to love You, and to follow You wholeheartedly. Help me to understand what it means to be washed thoroughly clean because of Your victory on the cross. Draw me close to You and fill me up until I'm spilling over with joy and health and a strong sense of Your goodness. Thank You for loving me like You do. You are everything to me. Amen.

Week 2

This Week's Disciplines

- *Rest Your Body (Allow 7 to 9 hours for night/bedtime routine)*
- *Rest Your Soul (Allow times for rest in God's presence)*

I truly believe that rest is the most underrated discipline of our day. We dip into our sleep time so we can get more done in a day, not realizing we're "robbing Peter to pay Paul." If we go too long without regular and consistent rest, it deeply impacts our health, perspective, and ability to live strong. When we de-prioritize rest, we make more mistakes, we use costly shortcuts, and we make ourselves more vulnerable to the enemy's schemes. It's critical that we prioritize rest, so here's what I'm asking you to do this week:

Make time and space in your evening for seven to nine hours of sleep. So let's say you have to wake up every morning at 6 a.m. For you to give yourself a seven- to nine-hour window, that means you need to start your night routine at 9 p.m. so you can be in bed by 10 p.m. This is the time to turn off your computer and TV and stop any work around the house. Hey, it's a perfect time to stretch! And pray! And read! Use that one-hour window to prepare your heart and mind for sleep. I'm telling you, this will be a very life-giving discipline.

Benefits of Sleep

- Body heals
- Stronger immune system
- Renewed perspective
- Higher ability to learn
- Less chance of mistakes
- Health maintenance

Spiritual Discipline: Cultivate a Restful Heart

Psalm 91:1 says this: "He who dwells in the secret place of the Most High shall abide under the shadow of the Almighty" (NKJV). What does it mean to *dwell in the secret place*? It's to walk in His presence as you live here on earth (see Psalm 116:9). It's to make time and space to meet with God, to listen for His voice, and to do what He says. It's to live with the sense that you're tucked under His protective wing, and to identify yourself as His with every step you take on planet earth. Now read that passage again: "He who dwells in the secret place of the Most High shall abide under the shadow of the Almighty." When you dwell with Him, you can more easily rest in Him. He has you, and is intimately acquainted with every detail of your life.

Here's another important verse: "Be still, and know that I am God" (Psalm 46:10). We get into striving and we work on overdrive when we forget that more is up to God than to us. The word *know* in this verse speaks of a single-minded intimacy (not allowing anything to get between you and God). Can you see why the enemy works overtime to distract you from the goodness and the greatness of our God? You're most powerful in your walk of faith and most restful amidst stressful circumstances when you know in your soul that He is God and that *you belong to Him.*

Learn to rest in Him. He loves you deeply.

I challenge you to make your nighttime routine a priority; get the sleep your body needs. That discipline will pay you back in great dividends!

I'll be praying for you as you add these healthy yet simple disciplines to your life.

Father,

Help me to establish a healthy rhythm in my life, both physically and spiritually. Help me to prioritize those things that make a world of difference in my life but that are just as easy to neglect. Remind me when it's time to stop working, turn off the TV or computer, and to meet with You before my head hits the pillow. Grant me deep and nourishing sleep and teach my heart while I rest in You. May I wake up each morning restored, healed, and refreshed. Help me to guard my heart against anxious thoughts and anxious ways. I have a tendency to let go of the things that nourish me and to do the things that weaken me. Forgive me, Lord! I want to lay hold of all You have for me: rest, strength, health, and abundant life. And it starts today. Lead me in the way that I should go. In Jesus' name I pray, Amen.

Week 3

This Week's Disciplines

- *Stand Up Straight*
- *Bow Low*

This week's discipline is easy to do and doesn't take a lot of effort, but it's even easier to forget about and neglect. How do you practice good posture? It's not hard at all. Right now sit up straight; pull your shoulders back, stretch your neck upright (like you're trying to add a couple inches to your height), pull in your abs (imagine pulling your navel all the way in until it touches your spine). When you stand, think *shoulders back and down, abs in, chest high, neck long—no slouching.*

We often slouch because we simply forget to stand up straight. But we sometimes slouch when we forget how important we are to God. One of my favorite passages of Scripture is 1 John 4:16: "And so we *know and rely* on the love God has for us." When we continually identify ourselves as loved by God and made in His image, we more instinctively carry ourselves with a holy confidence; we more readily understand that the power displayed in our lives comes from the treasure within. Determine to walk in a manner worthy of His name. Carry yourself like the heir you are!

Benefits of Good Posture

- Better for your frame (things are aligned; less stress on joints and muscles)
- Easier to breathe
- Makes you look 5 to 10 pounds lighter
- Reminds you to carry yourself with holy confidence

Spiritual Discipline: Bow Low (humble yourself)

First Peter 5:6–7 says this: "Humble yourselves, therefore, under God's mighty hand, that he may lift you up in due time. Cast all your anxiety on him because he cares for you."

More important than standing up straight is knowing when it's time to bow low. All too often we get it backward. We cower, buckle, and cover our heads when the enemy presses in hard to harass us. And when God moves in to correct or redirect, we tend to go rigid and be unteachable.

When the enemy presses in hard, though our instinct is to cower, our call is to stand fast, raise our shield, point our sword, and trust the Lord.

And when we approach the throne of almighty God, our call is to come humbly, reverently, and thankfully, because He is the star-breathing God who gladly welcomes us into His presence. To me, nothing stirs up my faith like pausing before I pray and remembering once again who God is, and marveling that He *invites me* to enjoy intimate fellowship *with Him*. I love to marvel, to stand in awe, and then to humbly bow, knowing that my life, my dreams, and my worries are all in His hands. He is God Most High, and I need Him every hour.

I encourage you to approach God with a new sense of reverence this week. I dare you to kneel or go facedown on the floor, not in dread or fear or with a worm-like mentality, but with a humble regard for His love and greatness. Scripture says that God considers the humble, contrite heart a lofty place to inhabit. Think about that for a moment: Our high and holy God considers our humble heart an honorable place to reside. We are blessed beyond measure, no?

Stand up straight with holy confidence and humbly bow with holy reverence—these are your two disciplines this week. I'll be praying for you as you add these two important disciplines to your life: Stand up straight in life and bow low before God.

Let's do this! May you flourish in health, both physically and spiritually.

Jesus,

Help me to remember once again who I am to You and who You are to me. I'm treasured beyond measure. I have every reason to walk and stand with a holy confidence because I belong to You! At yet, at the same time, I know that I'm nothing apart from you. I can accomplish no good thing unless You breathe life in and through my offering. And so I also bow low today. I open my hands and wait on You. Fill me afresh with the knowledge of You. Awaken my heart to live as one who is spoken for. I am Yours and You are mine. Your banner over me is Love. Thank you for this sacred invitation to intimate fellowship. You lead. I will follow. Amen.

Week 4

This Week's Disciplines

- *Work Your Heart*
- *Guard Your Heart*

Here's a discipline that will change your life if you'll make time for it! Give yourself permission to take doable steps. If you currently do no cardio exercise, pick two days this week to get out for a walk (or if the weather is less than ideal, go to the mall). Plan it on your calendar the way you schedule lunch with a friend. Make a date and keep it! Be sure to wear good athletic shoes that have great arch support (no flats, flip flops, etc.).

Start out slow and gradually pick up your pace until you feel challenged but can still carry on a conversation. That will put you in the aerobic zone (where you'll more easily burn fat, and more easily recover). Try to sustain this pace for thirty to forty-five minutes. Think about it: Giving yourself two hours this week to get your heart rate up and force your blood to circulate will do wonders for you. I'm telling you, eventually you won't want to give it up (you may even get cranky if you miss your cardio workout).

Ideally, if you can do a good cardio workout two to four times a week, you'll experience great health benefits. Give yourself permission to start small, but do start! That two- to four-hour investment will pay you back in huge dividends.

Benefits of Cardio

- Strengthens heart muscle
- Burns calories
- Relieves stress
- Improves circulation
- Renews perspective
- Maintains overall health

Spiritual Discipline: Guard Your Heart

Proverbs 4:23 says this: "Above all else, guard your heart, for everything you do flows from it."

As important as it is to work your heart doing cardio exercise, it's even more important that you guard your heart from influences that could derail your faith or diminish your impact. Picture a father on high alert who grabs a weapon to protect his home and family. He'll keep danger away from his family even if it costs him his own life. Now, this may sound dramatic, but that's how this verse translates.

God wants us to cherish our heart and the course of our lives with such care that we protect ourselves from toxic attitudes, unhealthy associations, and besetting sins. We need to treasure our life, our purpose, and our influence enough to carefully discern what strengthens us and what weakens us.

Spend some time this week searching your heart and dare to ask yourself the following questions:

- Am I holding on to grudges and judgments against others?
- Do I willingly expose myself to influences that I know are bad for me?
- Have I allowed jealousy, selfish ambition, or envy to cloud my view?
- Have I stopped being thankful?

If you can say yes to any of these questions, first of all, know that you are not alone! We all deal with these things and will continue to (in increasing measure) unless we guard our hearts. Spend some time with the Lord, and be specific in your prayers. Name the people you've judged and refused to forgive. Offer them up to the Lord. Ask His forgiveness for your unforgiveness. Ask Him to help you release the offense and embrace His promises instead. One by one, walk through these questions and answer them honestly before the Lord. Let Him take you by the hand and lead you to a place of refreshment and renewal. I promise you, He will.

Now it's time to change your ways! Turn to face God so he can wipe away your sins, pour out showers of blessing to refresh you, and send you the Messiah he prepared for you, namely, Jesus.

Acts 3:19 THE MESSAGE

I'll be praying for you as you add these two important disciplines to your life: working your heart and guarding your heart.

Let's do this! May you flourish in health, both physically and spiritually.

Here's a blessing for you:

May the Lord establish in you a healthy, divine rhythm of life. May He inspire you to make choices that are good and life-giving for you. May He strengthen you in mind, body, and spirit. Where you're broken, may He restore; where you're weary, may He refresh; where you're fearful, may He revive faith. May your coming days be far more blessed than your former days. Fully embrace this day! There'll be new mercies waiting for you in the morning.

Discipline Review (Through Week 4)

PHYSICAL DISCIPLINES

- Drink 8 to 10 glasses of water a day (or better yet, half of your body weight in ounces).
- Stretch in the morning and evening.
- Set aside 7 to 9 hours for nighttime rest/sleep.
- Work your heart.

SPIRITUAL DISCIPLINES

- Read the Word of God every day.
- Stretch your faith every day.

- Rest in the Lord.
- Guard your heart.

Week 5

This Week's Disciplines

- *Nourish Your Body*
- *Nourish Your Soul*

When was the last time you slowed down long enough to really *taste* your food? How often do you eat on the run? This week's discipline is all about presence, moderation, and variety. Here are a few tips to help you with physical nourishment:

- *Stay away from fad diets.* Think of healthy eating more as a lifestyle. If you view your current endeavor as a "diet," you'll eventually fall off your diet and may end up dealing with the self-condemnation that so often follows. One day at a time, sweet Jesus! Eat smaller portions and enjoy every bite.
- *Be present with God, with others, and with your food when you eat.* Take the time to thank God for the nourishment He provides. Slow down long enough to taste your food. Thank Him for friends and family and the freedom to enjoy them. Slow down and be present in the moment. Food, friends, and family are gifts from God.
- *Add color.* If you already enjoy plenty of fruits and vegetables, you're good to go. But if not, start here: add a piece of fruit and a side salad to your daily routine. Just that first step will strengthen your health and retrain your palette.
- *Wait for hunger pains*—listen to your body. Dr. Rita Hancock, author of *The Eden Diet*, suggests that unless we

actually feel hunger pangs at least twice a day, we're most likely overeating. Don't force your body to abide by an imposed schedule. Follow its rhythm and you'll feel much better. Do what you can to accommodate your hunger in a healthy way, and any excess weight will most likely melt away!

- *Budget treats.* Have your treats, but plan for them! If you eat a chocolate bar while hiding in the closet, it's still fattening. So eat a few bites out in the open and save the rest for later!

- *Practice partial fasts.* Every day, a couple times a day, say no to yourself and make yourself deal with it. Don't give in to every hunger whim you experience. It's good for your body and good for your soul when you exercise some kind of self-restraint on a regular basis.

Spiritual Discipline: Be Nourished

Just as we acquire a taste for healthy nourishment, we also acquire a taste for spiritual nourishment. The more we feed on the Word of God, the greater capacity we have to be nourished by it.

- *Keep it colorful.* With the exception of Scripture, don't overload on only once choice of nourishment (one musician, one preacher, one author, etc.). Jesus has equipped a multitude of His children to build up His kingdom. When you feast on the fruit of only one of His servants, you run the risk of becoming narrow in your thinking and acceptance of how things should be communicated. Scripture says there's wisdom in many counselors.

- *Take responsibility for your spiritual health.* It's not your pastor's job, or your spouse's job, or your friend's job to keep you on track. Love your life and your calling enough to dig into the Word and to listen for God's voice, no matter what. Be so rooted in Jesus that if the whole world around you shakes, you'll still be standing when it's all said and done.

- *Be present with God.* Scripture says it's in His presence that the fullness of joy is found (Psalm 16:11). When you sit down for soul nourishment, pause and think about who it is you're connected to. You're connected to the living God! The One who put the mountains in place knows your name and loves you deeply. Read the Word and pray as someone who is deeply loved, profoundly called, and wonderfully equipped.[2]

Lord Jesus,
Give me a renewed love for my life and my calling and inspire me to care for my body and my soul. Increase my hunger and thirst for times in Your presence, times in Your Word. Give me a taste for all that's good for me, and help me to lose the taste for all that diminishes me. I am Yours and You are mine. Your banner over me is love. Help me to live as one who is spoken for. My life matters, thanks to You. Amen.

Week 6

This Week's Disciplines

- *Stretch Your Muscles*
- *Stretch Your Faith*

I'm telling you, friend, if you take a few moments every morning and every evening to stretch your major muscle groups, you'll feel a whole lot better and carry yourself taller! Here are some of the many benefits of stretching regularly:

- Alleviates most body aches
- Reduces stress
- Improves circulation
- Increases overall flexibility
- Reduces occurrence of injury

Dangers of NOT stretching:

- Higher level of muscle discomfort
- Greater potential of injury
- Decreased circulation
- Increase of muscle/joint issues
- Absorb stress in a way that diminishes health

When you roll out of bed in the morning, face your mirror, stand with your feet shoulder-width apart, and bend your knees slightly (sit back slightly in squat position; shift weight to your heels). Place your left hand on your left thigh and stretch your right hand in the air (pointing upward—12:00). With knees still bent and your left hand on your left thigh for support, and abs tight to support your lower back, gently stretch that arm overhead until you're pointing 11 or 10:00). Then repeat on the other side. Lie on the floor, put your hands under your knees, and gently pull them toward your chest. If you're able, extend one leg in the air and stretch your hamstring; flex and point your toe to get that lower leg warmed up as well. (Then repeat with the other side.) Stand up and take a few deep breaths by breathing in through the nose and exhaling through the mouth. Doing a few basic stretches like these will energize you and help you feel ready for your day! It's amazing what a difference a few moments of stretching will do for you. Repeat this routine again at night before you go to bed. If you need more instruction when it comes to stretching, you'll find a number of instructional videos on YouTube.

Spiritual Discipline: Stretch Your Faith

Scripture says that we cannot please God without faith! So this week it's time to activate your faith in a more intentional way. *Each day this week,* ask the Lord to show you what He wants you to believe Him for (Is it rest? Provision? Direction? A future promised land?). Then start thanking Him by faith for His promise to you. Find a Scripture to stand on and start living like His promises are true!

Also, make yourself available to Him each and every day. *Ask Him to use you in ways that surprise you.* Pay attention to that inner nudge and move when He tells you to move. Buy a cup of coffee for someone in need. Write a letter. Open a door. Reach out to a stranger. Listen for the Lord's voice and then do what He says. Your faith is precious and priceless to Him!

Here's why stretching our faith is so important to us:

- Reminds us of who (and Whose) we are
- We grow in the things of God
- We become spiritually conditioned to take the land God wants to give us
- Reminds us that we're pilgrims on this earth, just passing through
- Reminds us that greater is He who is in us, than he who is in the world
- We bring pleasure to God's heart when we live by faith

Scriptures for faith stretching:

What good is it, my brothers and sisters, if someone claims to have faith but has no deeds? Can such faith save them?

James 2:14

For we live by faith, not by sight.

2 Corinthians 5:7

Dangers of living an earthbound life:

- We lose our sense of expectancy
- We lose sight of our invitation to walk intimately with God
- We miss out on an exciting faith adventure
- We're easily deceived by the enemy
- We settle for far less than what God has for us

I'll be praying for you as you add these healthy yet simple disciplines to your life. May you flourish in health, both physically and spiritually!

Jesus, thank you for Your goodness to me! Forgive me for sometimes making an idol out of my own comfort. I'm ready to be stretched in a way that grows my faith and reflects Your grace in my life. I make myself available to You this day. Open my eyes to see who You've appointed me to bless today! Give me a heart to step out in faith and to reach out in love. Increase Your territory in and through me, and make me more like You. In Jesus' name, I pray. Amen.

Discipline Review

PHYSICAL DISCIPLINES

- Drink 8 to 10 glasses of water a day (or better yet, half of your body weight in ounces).
- Stretch in the morning and evening.
- Set aside 7 to 9 hours for nighttime rest/sleep.
- Work your heart.
- Nourish your body.
- Stand tall.

SPIRITUAL DISCIPLINES

- Read the Word of God every day.
- Stretch your faith every day.
- Rest in the Lord.
- Guard your heart.
- Nourish your soul.
- Bow low.

Acknowledgments

To these dear friends, colleagues, and family members, I offer my most sincere, heartfelt thanks:

Leslie Wilson, thank you for your input, advice, and direction on this project. Having you with me on this journey was priceless to me! Bless you!

Andy McGuire, you are more than an editor, you are an intelligent, wonderful man of God. Thank you for seeing and embracing the value of this message and for shepherding me through the process of this book. I'm so very grateful to you and the whole Bethany House family. Thank you, too, Jeff Braun, Carra Carr, and Erin Hollister. Your kingdom hearts shine bright!

Steve Laube, you're a wonderful literary agent. I've deeply benefited from your wisdom, experience, and insight. Thank you for being awesome. Appreciate you so very much!

Maria Yates, bless you for managing my speaking schedule. You've been kind, patient, and sooo understanding when I've had to say no (which is often, I know). I can't tell you what it means to me that you care about my schedule and that I keep a sustainable pace. I thank God for you!

Dick Whitworth, Neil Stavem, Matt Reynolds, Grace Reif, and the rest of the Faith Radio team. I don't have enough room on this page to express my heart for you! I'm so honored to daily serve the Lord alongside you. We've seen God do great things in our midst. And with all my heart I believe that greater things are still to be done here! Bless you.

My sample readers: Meredith Andrews, Daryl Jackson, Lynn Ferguson, Cynthia Fantasia, Bonnie Costello, Cindy Larson, Kathy Schwanke, Andi Munn, Kay Blake, Bonnie Newberg, Susan Stuart, Kelly Black, Karen Telle, Stephanie Johnson, Pamela Nelson, Ellen Habeck, Barb Odom, Tamra Peterson, Jill Schoolmeesters, Jane Bjork, Patty Fischer, Petra Krebbs, Cindy Hall, Andrea Caniff, Janet Krekelberg, Theresa Carlson, Cheri Hahn, and Jeanne Burgbacher. Thank you for taking the time to read through my rough drafts, for sharing your insights, and for encouraging me along the way. Bless you, girls!

My intercessors: Both Kev and I thank you from the bottoms of our hearts for the way you go to battle for us. Your prayers have made a difference in our lives time and time again. We've noticed tangible changes in our circumstances after we've asked you to pray. May the Lord release fresh favor over your lives for your investment in ours! Bless you and thank you.

Tom and Cindy Hall, thank you for showing up to pull weeds while I worked to finish this book. I'm still overwhelmed at the thought of you out there working up a sweat. How can I ever say thank you for your kindness to us? We love and appreciate you so much!

Mom, Gary, Greg, Pam, Jeff, Karen, and Krissy, thank you for allowing me to share Dad's story. I know those hours before he passed were sacred to all of us. May we all live with eternity in mind. Love you so much.

Jake and Lizzie, Luke and Kristen, Jordan and Anita, we love you more than we can express. The deepest desire of our hearts is that you'll grasp, more and more, how deeply God loves you, and that you'll live in response to the *finished* work of Christ. You've got nothing to prove and all of eternity to live for. May your yeses and no's be set apart for Him. You're so precious to us!

Kevin, may God take the prayers we pray every morning and every night and do above and beyond all we could ever dare to ask or imagine . . . just like He said He would. My faith and expectancy grow every time we pray. I don't want to do this journey with anybody but you. Love you with all my heart.

Jesus, I owe my whole life to You. I marvel that You saved me. I humbly bow before You, open my hands, and give You this offering from the depths of my heart. May Your best will be done with this book. I pray You'll do a miracle in the lives of every precious soul who works their way through these pages. May they reclaim their days and their commitments in a way that strengthens them. May they enjoy a fresh intimacy with You like they've never known before. And may they find joy, purpose, and passion with every step they take until they see You face-to-face. Thank You, Lord, for allowing me to steward this message. You are the King of my heart.

Notes

Chapter 1: Caution: Danger Ahead

1. Beth Moore, *When Godly People Do Ungodly Things* (Nashville: B&H Publishers, 2002), 56.
2. Tim Chester, *The Busy Christian's Guide to Busyness* (Nottingham, England: InterVarsity Press, 2006), 77–78.
3. Moore, *When Godly People Do Ungodly Things*, 177.
4. L. B. Cowman, *Streams in the Desert* (Grand Rapids, MI: Zondervan, 1997), 477 (emphasis mine).

Chapter 2: When I Move Too Fast

1. Mark Buchanan, *The Rest of God* (Nashville: W Publishing Group, 2006), 1–2.
2. Kevin DeYoung, *Crazy Busy* (Wheaton, IL: Crossway, 2013), 30.
3. William MacDonald, *Believer's Bible Commentary* (Nashville: Thomas Nelson Publishers, 1980), 1930.

Chapter 3: Busyness vs. Abundance

1. Bruce Wilkinson, *You Were Born for This* (Colorado Springs, CO: Multnomah Publishers, 2009), 32.
2. Ibid.
3. Caroline also makes this statement in her book *Willing to Walk on Water* (Carol Stream, IL: Tyndale House Publishers, 2013).
4. My friend Joanna Weaver coined the phrase "fill and spill."
5. MacDonald, *Believer's Bible Commentary*, 1919.

Chapter 4: There's Rest in God's Yes

1. Alan Fadling, *An Unhurried Life* (Downers Grove, IL: InterVarsity Press, 2013), 16.

2. Ibid., 96.

3. John Ortberg, *Soul Keeping* (Grand Rapids, MI: Zondervan, 2013), 85.

4. Dallas Willard quote from John Ortberg's book *Soul Keeping* (Grand Rapids, MI: Zondervan, 2013), 10.

Chapter 5: Am I Captive?

1. David Lomas, *The Truest Thing About You* (Colorado Springs, CO: David C. Cook, 2014), 21, 33.

2. Questions paraphrased from Edward T. Welch, *When People Are Big and God Is Small* (Phillipsburg, NJ: P&R Publishing, 1997), 15–16.

3. Lomas, *The Truest Thing About You*, 193.

4. Elyse Fitzpatrick, *Found in Him* (Wheaton, IL: Crossway, 2013), 83, 93, emphasis mine.

Chapter 6: The Power of Peer Pressure

1. Edward T. Welch, *When People Are Big and God Is Small* (Phillipsburg, NJ: P&R Publishing, 1997), 40.

2. Welch, *When People Are Big and God Is Small*, 19.

3. Andrew Murray, *Humility* (Minneapolis, MN: Bethany House, 2001), 80.

4. John Fischer, *12 Steps for the Recovering Pharisee* (Minneapolis, MN: Bethany House, 2000), 49.

Chapter 7: Do You See What He Sees?

1. Brady Boyd, *Sons & Daughters* (Grand Rapids, MI: Zondervan, 2012), 67.

2. Elizabeth Barrett Browning, "Aurora Leigh," *Seventh Book* (London: J. Miller, 1864), emphasis mine.

3. Emily Freeman, *A Million Little Ways* (Grand Rapids, MI: Revell, 2013), 72, 84.

4. Eugene Peterson's Message translation of Hebrews 6:13–18.

5. Warren Wiersbe, *The Wiersbe Bible Commentary (NT)* (Colorado Springs, CO: David C. Cook, 2007), 819.

6. Boyd, *Sons & Daughters*, 67.

7. Adapted from Susie Larson, *The Uncommon Woman* (Chicago: Moody Publishers, 2008), 26.

Chapter 8: There's Freedom in God's Yes

1. Lomas, *The Truest Thing About You*, 27.

2. Will Davis Jr., *10 Things Jesus Never Said* (Grand Rapids, MI: Revell, 2011), 109.

Chapter 9: When God Redirects

1. DeYoung, *Crazy Busy*, 58.

2. R. T. Kendall, *These Are the Days of Elijah* (Bloomington, MN: Chosen Books, 2013), 89.

3. Henry Cloud, *Necessary Endings* (New York: Harper Collins, 2010), 81–82.

4. L. B. Cowman, *Streams in the Desert* (Grand Rapids, MI: Zondervan, 1997), 250.

5. Charles and Janet Morris, *Missing Jesus* (Chicago: Moody Publishers, 2014), 174.

Chapter 10: Simple Sacred Steps

1. Richard Swenson, *Margin* (Colorado Springs, CO: NavPress, 1992), 222.

2. Wiersbe, *The Wiersbe Bible Commentary (NT)*, 817.

3. Rick Renner, *Sparkling Gems From the Greek* (Tulsa, OK: Teach All Nations, 2003), 130–131.

4. DeYoung, *Crazy Busy*, 118.

Chapter 11: Stand in Power

1. William L. Ford, III, *Created for Influence* (Grand Rapids, MI: Chosen Books, 2007), 63.

2. Wilkinson, *You Were Born for This*, 43.

3. Studylight.org, HCS translation, Thayer-Strong's study note on 2 Timothy 1:7.

4. Wiersbe, *The Wiersbe Bible Commentary (NT)*, 773.

5. Studylight.org, HCS translation, Thayer-Strong's study note on 2 Timothy 1:7.

6. Larson, *The Uncommon Woman*, 49.

7. *New Spirit-Filled Life Bible (NKJV)* (Nashville: Thomas Nelson, 2002), 1711, 2 Timothy 1:7 study note.

8. Jeff Kinley, *As It Was in the Days of Noah* (Eugene, OR: Harvest House, 2014), 75.

9. Renner, *Sparkling Gems From the Greek*, 997.

Chapter 12: Closing Thoughts

1. Susie Larson, *Balance That Works When Life Doesn't* (Eugene, OR: Harvest House Publishers, 2005), 221.

2. Lisa Bevere, *Lioness Arising* (Colorado Springs, CO: Waterbrook Press, 2010), 76, emphasis mine.

Chapter 13: Bonus Chapter

1. Larson, *The Uncommon Woman*, 183.

2. Tips adapted from my book, *Balance That Works When Life Doesn't*.

Susie Larson is a popular radio host, national speaker, and author. She hosts a daily radio talk show, *Live the Promise with Susie Larson*. Her passion is to see men and women everywhere strengthened in their faith and mobilized to live out their high calling in Jesus Christ.

Her eight previous books include *Your Beautiful Purpose*, *Growing Grateful Kids*, and *The Uncommon Woman*.

Susie and her husband, Kevin, live near Minneapolis, Minnesota, and have three adult sons, three beautiful daughters-in-law, and one adorable pit bull. For more information, visit www.susielarson.com.

Dig Deeper Into
Your Sacred Yes

Whether you're reading *Your Sacred Yes* on your own or within a Bible study group, get the most out of your study with these additional resources!

Download the FREE Workbook From SusieLarson.com

The *Your Sacred Yes* workbook goes beyond the Reflection Questions provided in the book, connecting the message to additional Scripture passages and inviting you to think more deeply about how to apply what you've learned to your life.

Host a Six-Week Study

Let Susie guide your group with this DVD Study Companion, which includes six thirty-minute segments that cover and expand on the material in the book, two chapters at a time.

Connect With Susie

Visit SusieLarson.com to subscribe to her newsletter
and learn about her upcoming speaking engagements.
You can also connect with her on Facebook and Twitter.

 deeperlifeinchrist  @SusieLarson

---

 "Live the Promise"
With Susie Larson

Susie's radio show offers inspiration and insight for living
a deeper life in Christ and a more powerful life on earth.
The goal of "Live the Promise" is to encourage and strengthen
your faith through conversations that bring Scripture to life,
practical ideas to live out your convictions, and stories that will
inspire you to hang on when life is hard.

Tune in online or find a signal in your area at
MyFaithRadio.com/programs/live-the-promise/

Available From
Susie Larson

Visit SusieLarson.com for more information.

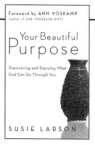